MEL BAY'S
complete irish flute Book

by
Mizzy McCaskill
& Dona Gilliam

Cover Design by Wade Lough, Graphic Designer
Photography by DeeDee Niarhos, Mount Crawford, VA

ONLINE AUDIO

1. **The Drunken Sailor,** hornpipe [3:20]

2. **King of the Fairies,** set dance [3:51]
   The Ships are Sailing, reel
   The Mason's Apron, reel

3. **Sloan's Lamentation,** air [4:22]
   Julia McMahon, jig
   Come Along With Me, jig
   The Lovely Lad, jig

4. **Tipperary Hills,** jig [2:40]
   The Jolly Corkonian, jig
   Jackson's Bottle of Brandy, jig

5. **The Bloom of Youth,** reel [2:09]
   Touch Me If You Dare, reel
   The Blackberry Blossom, reel

6. **General Monroe's Lamentation,** air [4:09]
   Wellington's Advance, jig
   The Rambler from Clare, jig

7. **The Woods of Kilmurry,** air [3:52]
   The Red Haired Hag, jig
   (C Flute and Alto Flute)
      Sax: Gunnar Mossblad
      Bass: John C. Fishell

8. **Lord Mayo,** air [4:42]
   Behind the Bush in the Garden, jig
   The Humours of Ballinafauna, jig
      Sax: Gunnar Mossblad

9. **Twas on a Winter's Evening,** song [5:53]
      Guitar: John C. Fishell
      Voice: Mizzy McCaskill

10. **Banish Misfortune,** jig [4:21]
    Galway Tom, jig

11. **The Winter it is Past,** song [5:15]
       Voice: Mizzy McCaskill

To Access the Online Audio Go To:
www.melbay.com/96332MEB

1 2 3 4 5 6 7 8 9 0

Visit us on the Web at www.melbay.com — E-mail us at email@melbay.com

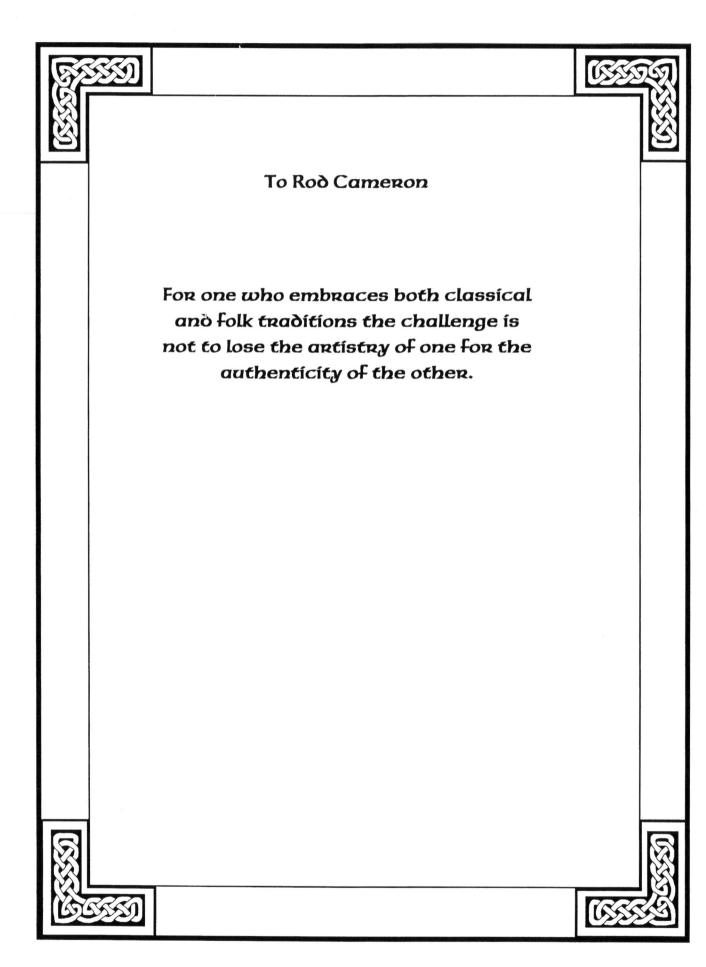

To Rod Cameron

For one who embraces both classical
and folk traditions the challenge is
not to lose the artistry of one for the
authenticity of the other.

Contents

I.	Historical Notes	4-8
II.	Fundamentals	9-10
	Hand Position	9
	Finger Position	9
	Embouchure	10
	Breath Support	10
III.	Irish Music	11-18
	Jigs	12-14
	Hornpipe	15
	Reel	16
	Set Dance	17-18
IV.	Performance Practice	19-24
	Tempo	20
	Rhythm	20
	Phrasing	20-22
	Breath Support	23-24
	Ornamentation	25-127
	Slide	26-28
	Cut	29
	Cuts (Fingering Chart)	30-31
	Cuts Between Two Notes of the Same Pitch (Fingering Chart)	32-36
	Pieces for Study of Cuts	37-47
	Double Grace Notes	48
	Scale Practice for Double Grace Notes	48-52
	Pieces for Study of Double Grace Notes	53-59
	Triple Grace Notes	60-61
	Triplets	62-66
	Rolls	67-125
	Short Roll	67
	Short Roll Fingerings	68-70
	Short Roll Exercises	71-76
	Pieces for Study of Short Rolls	77-99
	Long Roll	100
	Long Roll Fingerings	101-103
	Long Roll Exercises	104-107
	Pieces for Study of Long Rolls	108-125
	Cran	126-127
	Process of Variation	128-130
	Styles	131-133
V.	Slow Airs and Songs	134-142
	Vibrato	134
	Diaphragmatic Vibrato	135
	Fingered Vibrato	136
VI.	Pieces for Study and Practice	143-163
	Piano Accompaniments	164-179
VII.	Fingering Charts	180-188
VIII.	Indexes	189-192

The Irish flute is a term which alternately means a flute played in the Irish style, the type of simple system or keyless wooden instrument favored by flutists who play Irish folk music, or instruments played in Irish flute bands. The historical development of the flute most accurately depicts how the various forms of the Irish flute came into existence, hence a brief overview follows.

This overview will begin with the Baroque flute (also called a traverso) that enjoyed popularity in the late seventeenth through mid-eighteenth centuries. Early flutes were fashioned from wood, and it is easy to assume that any wooden flute is suitable for playing in the Irish style. This is not the case. Baroque flutes had a mellow, soft tone that is generally not acceptable for performing in the Irish style. Reproductions of these early flutes are widely available hence some confusion may exist regarding their suitability for use in the Irish folk idiom. All wooden flutes do not have the same playing characteristics, therefore it is important to understand the differences among early instruments.

Baroque flutes generally have a cylindrical head, cylindrical/conical joint(s) with finger holes, and a foot joint with one key. Flutes of the Baroque era were made in different keys and sizes, although the more common varieties would sound the note 'D' when all of the tone holes were covered. This note in all probability would sound below current-day standards for a 'D' concert pitch, but it is used as a reference point from which to discuss the range of the instrument.

A chromatic scale could be played on the Baroque-style flute with the use of half-holing and cross-fingering (fingering in which open holes alternated with closed holes). A chart of fingerings for the Baroque-style flute is shown on the next page. Keep in mind that fingerings vary considerably according to the unique acoustical properties of each instrument, and that the chart represents one set of possible fingerings.

Early flutes had many shortcomings that would eventually lead to the development of more refined flute mechanisms: they were invariably out of tune, their tone quality was not consistent throughout the range of the instrument, and they required technical facility to play a full compass of keys.

**Baroque, one-keyed flute after G.A. Rottenburgh, circa 1750.
Rod Cameron, maker.**

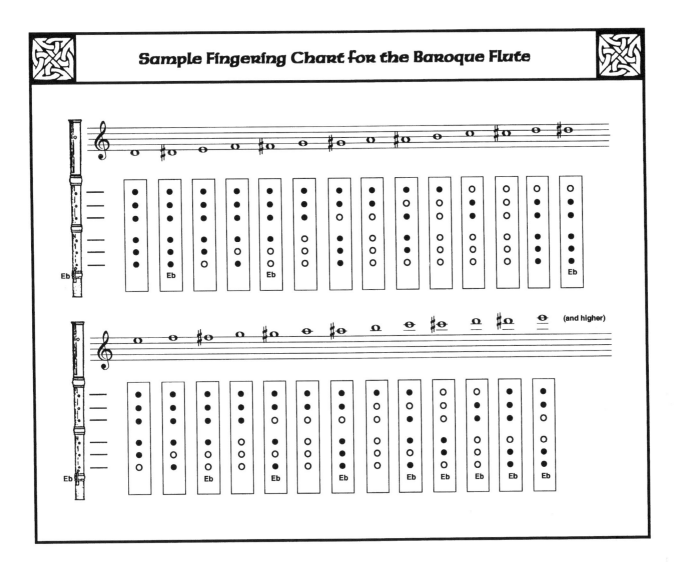

In the mid-eighteenth century flute makers began to experiment with additional keywork in order to improve upon the technical facility and intonation offered by the one-keyed flute.

Flute with four keys

By the late nineteenth century flutes with as many as eight keys were accepted as alternatives to the older one-keyed instruments. Numerous labels are attached to these multiple-keyed instruments from *German* to *old system* to *simple system* (meaning flutes made prior to the advent of the Boehm system).

Flute with eight keys

Other important modifications were made to keyed flutes during this evolutionary period: tone holes and embouchure holes were enlarged for a more powerful sound, metal slides were inserted into the headpiece for increased volume and ease of tuning, and exotic woods (granadilla, rosewood, etc.) were used for improved tone quality. Many of these new and improved simple system flutes may be considered Irish flutes in the hands of a traditional player.

While professional instrument makers/players sought to improve upon the flute mechanism, folk musicians adapted to the idiosyncrasies of simple system flutes. Traditional Irish dance music originating in the eighteenth and nineteenth centuries would have been played by an ensemble of folk instruments popular at the time (e.g. fiddle, pipes, and accordion). Since folk music was generally played and transcribed in the keys of D, G, or A with related modalities the fingerings of simple system flutes were ideally suited to the demands of the folk genre. Extra key mechanisms became superfluous even though flutes were designed to play chromatically. Most of the keywork on older instruments is not employed by the traditional player in the context of traditional Irish dance music. A keyless wooden flute with enlarged tone holes is favored by most contemporary folk flutists as the instrument of choice for playing traditional Irish music.

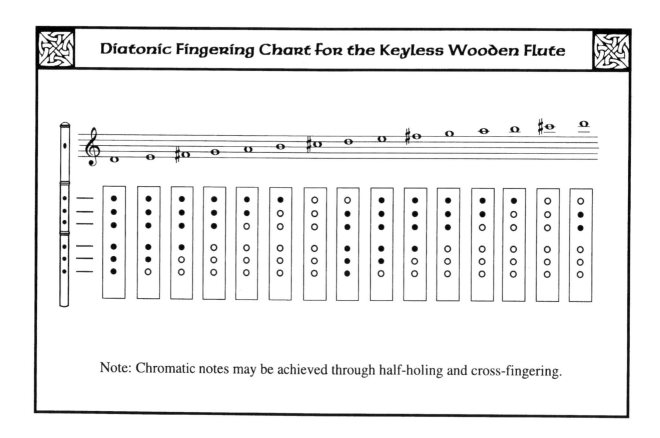

Diatonic Fingering Chart for the Keyless Wooden Flute

Note: Chromatic notes may be achieved through half-holing and cross-fingering.

Folk musicians have not always been in a position to purchase an instrument of their choice. They have relied instead upon instruments handed down from previous generations or those made by local craftsmen. This is one reason why the preference for older style wooden flutes was retained by many players even though the instrument underwent radical changes in the mid-nineteenth century.

The introduction of Theobald Boehm's flute design of 1847 was to revolutionize flute playing and manufacturing. The silver Boehm flute set the standard for professional and student lines of flutes for band and orchestral players, and over the years the wooden flute was relegated to folk musicians and performers on period instruments. Folk musicians continued to play older instruments despite the improvements offered by the Boehm system, and the wooden simple system flute is still preferred by most traditional players. The chart on the following page lists differences between the Boehm (silver) flute and the keyless Irish flute.

Although the Boehm flute is not a traditional Irish flute it may be played in the Irish style. Some traditional players have adapted to the Boehm flute as a matter of convenience. Antique instruments in good repair are difficult to find, and wooden instruments require careful attention and maintenance. The silver flute, on the other hand, is readily available. It plays well in tune and carries well in the group setting. The spirit of the music reigns in the end, and the subtleties involved in the choice of an instrument are a matter of personal preference.

The historical evolution of the Irish flute must make mention of Irish flute bands that originated in Northern Ireland as an outgrowth of British army bands in the nineteenth century. These groups marched at festive occasions with ensembles of flutes and drums. Their instrumentation included a full range of keyed wooden-instruments ranging from various sizes of piccolos and flutes to alto and bass flutes (the latter two fashioned of metal). As the Boehm flute became standard, flute bands began to incorporate contemporary instruments into their ensembles: C piccolos, C concert, G alto, and C bass flutes. An additional G treble flute is unique to flute bands as it has never been widely popularized outside of Ireland and the British Isles.

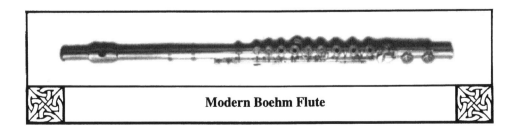

Modern Boehm Flute

A Comparison of Features

Keyless Wooden Flute

- no lip plate

- tone hole placement may cause awkward finger stretches

- intonation requires adjustment through the octaves

- mellow sound due to resonant properties of wood

- small dynamic range

- more appropriate for use with traditional ornamentation such as the slide

- player may comfortably access the keys of D, G, and A (with related modalities)

Boehm Silver Flute

(French open-hole model shown here; closed-hole models are also available)

- raised lip plate to aid in direction of air stream and playing comfort

- key mechanism eliminates awkward stretches and provides full chromatic range

- better intonation throughout range of instrument due to acoustically correct placement of tone holes

- tonal brilliance due to metal tube and enlarged tone holes

- capable of fuller dynamic range

- slide ornamentation effective only on open-hole models

- provides full access to all major and minor keys with use of chromatic key mechanism

This edition of *Mel Bay's Complete Irish Flute Book* will present a method for learning to ornament the **Boehm** flute in the Irish style. The Boehm flute is the standard silver flute that enjoys widespread use as a band and orchestral instrument today, and the keywork on the Boehm flute requires different fingerings than simple system flutes. Players wishing to learn Irish ornamentation on simple system or keyless wooden flutes are advised to follow the fingering and pedagogy presented for the tin whistle in *Mel Bay's Complete Irish Tin Whistle Book*. The tin whistle is often used as a starter instrument for the flute, and its fingering is very similar to that used for most keyless wooden flutes.

This book also requires familiarity with conventional music notation and an ability to sound and finger the Boehm flute. For assistance in learning to play the flute consult these other Mel Bay Publications: *The Flutist's Companion; The Flute Handbook;* and *Indispensable Scales, Exercises, and Etudes for the Developing Flutist.*

The ![symbol] symbol will be used throughout this text to indicate those pieces which have been recorded on the accompanying CD. Recorded dance tunes are usually repeated two or three times. The articulation markings given for each piece approximate closely the articulations used the first time each tune is played. Variations may occur on subsequent repetitions.

Fundamentals

The following material assumes that the reader is familiar with the hand position, embouchure (formation of lips), tonguing, and breath support used when playing the Boehm flute (silver flute). A comparison of techniques used by players on wooden flutes will give the classically trained flutist an idea of the acceptable variations used by players in the folk genre.

Hand Position

Hand position on the Boehm flute can vary considerably from that used by the traditional folk player. The classically trained flutist balances the flute on the left-hand (the joint between the index finger and palm), with the thumb of the right hand acting as another strategic balance point.

Wooden flute players may use the classical hand position, but they might also vary the left hand position. Alternative hand positions may require the rotation of flute joints to accomodate different balance points. Often times the resultant right hand position requires the right arm to be raised higher than the position used by the Boehm player. The physical size of the player as well as the tone-hole placement on the particular instrument determine appropriate hand positions for the folk player.

Finger Position

The fingers should be gently curved over the keys for proper fingering of Boehm flutes.

Curved Fingers

Players on wooden flutes often use flat-fingered playing technique. For some it is a transition from playing the pipes, where the middle/joint area of the finger rather than the pad of the finger is used to cover the tone hole. For others it is necessitated by the size of the tone holes.

Flat Fingers

Flat-fingered position is not a requirement for playing in the Irish style on wooden or Boehm flutes. The closed-hole Boehm flute may also be played in this manner, but the classically trained player will probably prefer to keep the fingers in a gently curved position for maximum ease of playing.

The structure of the French open-hole model flute makes flat-fingering difficult. The rod mechanism prevents the player from covering open holes adequately and it is more secure to use the pads of the fingers to cover the tone holes.

Flat-fingering on the Boehm flute is also likely to damage the rod mechanism or cause the flute to need frequent adjustment for the key pads to sit properly.

Embouchure

The embouchure used by folk players varies from player to player. It is not necessary for the classically trained player to change the embouchure to play in the Irish style. It is important to note, however, that the player of the wooden flute must achieve a biting, crisp, and piercing sound to be heard in a group of players or above sounds generated by dancers. The variation in tone color that the classical player achieves through control over the embouchure and mouth cavity is not as important to the traditional Irish player. In order to achieve a piercing sound, the traditional player will often turn the headjoint inwards to cover more of the embouchure hole with the lower lip. This achieves what is referred to in classical circles as an 'edgy' sound. Boehm flutists can achieve the same focused sound in one of two ways: by adjusting the embouchure to direct more air into the flute, or by turning the headjoint inwards to realign the flute.

Tonguing

In the classical tradition the use of the tongue is imperative for precise articulation. In the aural tradition of Irish flute playing the sound achieved on the instrument is more important than the manner of production. Articulation is often achieved through fingering/ornamentation as opposed to the tongue. Many traditional players use the tip of the tongue when articulating (as if to whisper the word 'too'). Others make use of a breath attack alone. This can be combined with a glottal articulation using a 'k' sound or the back of the throat (as if clearing the throat). The classically trained player is advised to continue using standard tonguing with the tip of the tongue, as the differences obtained by other means are minimal.

Breath Support

The manner in which the breath is controlled by the player contributes to a 'traditional Irish flute sound. Traditional players value the loudness and carrying power of a tone, and this requires a forceful stream of air. This is especially true for those playing instruments with large embouchure holes.

The diaphragmatic support employed by classically trained players is helpful in sustaining a forceful air stream and the same support mechanism is used by traditional players. Subtleties of the support mechanism such as the tapering of the air stream at phrase endings and dynamic contrasts are generally not observed in the folk tradition. More often than not traditional players will highlight the end of a piece with an accentuated push of air from the diaphragm.

The classically trained player also uses diaphragmatic support to create vibrato (the wavering or pulsation of a tone used to add color and motion to a musical line). Vibrato, if used at all by traditional players, is employed in slow airs (see section discussing slow airs). It is usually accomplished by wavering the fingers over open tone holes as opposed to pulsating the air stream with the aid of the diaphragm or throat musculature. This is not always the case; however, a more traditional sound can be achieved when playing dance music if the diaphragmatic vibrato is not used.

Some traditional players also use a pulsation or thrust of air from the diaphragm in conjunction with the meter of a piece. The accentuation of a rhythmic pulse can also be heard in performances by other instrumentalists. Fiddle players accentuate meter and rhythm by varying pressure with the bow arm, and accordion players give a noticeable push or pull of air through the reed of the instrument. There is not a set rule or convention for the application of this technique, but its use can impart a very traditional feel to the performance of dance music.

Irish music

The bulk of traditional Irish folk music consists of dance tunes and airs that date from the seventeenth to nineteenth centuries. Many of the dance tunes (especially jigs and hornpipes) adhere to a sixteen measure, binary (two-part) form. The first eight measures (A section) are known as the *tune*, and the second eight measures (B section) are known as the *turn*. Note the formal markings in the following jig:

Miss Grant's Jig

As in the above example, each section of the music is usually repeated (doubled). If a section has similar phrases (exact repetitions), it may be played only one time through (singled). This is more common in reels where a three part ABA or ABC form is often the standard. Entire pieces are repeated many times in the dance setting until the dance concludes. In solo performances of jigs, reels, and hornpipes, each piece is repeated two or three times and is usually linked to other dances of the same type.

Beyond large formal structures, specific dance types have distinguishing characteristics.

Jigs

There are three varieties of the jig: the **double jig** in $\frac{6}{8}$ time, the **single jig** in $\frac{6}{8}$ or $\frac{12}{8}$ time, and the **hop jig** (also called a **slip jig**) in $\frac{9}{8}$ time.

Double Jig

The **double jig** is delineated from other jigs by its characteristic rhythm of repeated eighth notes:

(At the player's discretion, repeated eighth notes may also be interpreted with a   rhythm.)

The A and B sections of the double jig will use the running eighth note figure predominantly throughout, with the last bar changing to:

The last measure frequently repeats the tonic note, and the most common ending will repeat the tonic on the last two or three notes of the piece. This is seen in the following double jig:

The Connachtman's Rambles

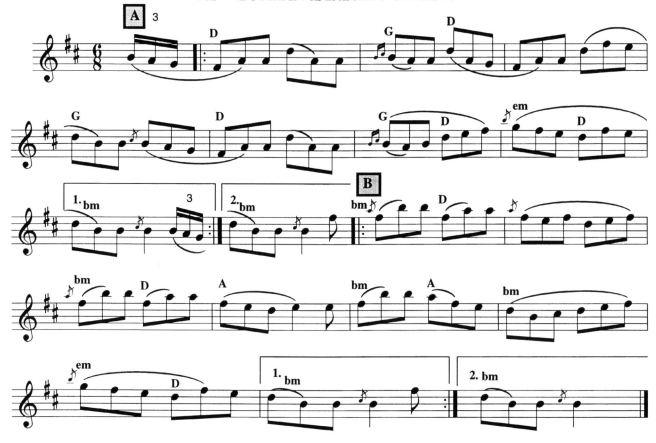

 # Single Jig

The **single jig** incorporates more ♩ ♪♩ ♪ rhythms in its A and B sections

than the double jig. The last bar of each section often ends on a final ♩. ♩ rhythm.

This can be seen in the following single jig:

The Shady Lane

Slip Jig

The **slip** or **hop jig** uses various groupings of ♩♪♪♪ , ♩ ♪ , and ♩. rhythms.

It is distinguished by its 9/8 time signature.

A large number of Irish dance tunes end on a note designed to lead into another strain or to a repeated section. The performer wishing to end a piece written in this manner will appropriately select the tonic as the final note of resolution. Note how the following slip jig requires some reworking to this effect. Different endings can be added by the performer. An extra measure can be tagged on at the end, or the final few notes of the piece may be rewritten until they comfortably resolve to the tonic. A suggested ending that resolves to tonic is given for the following slip jig:

Comb Your Hair and Curl It

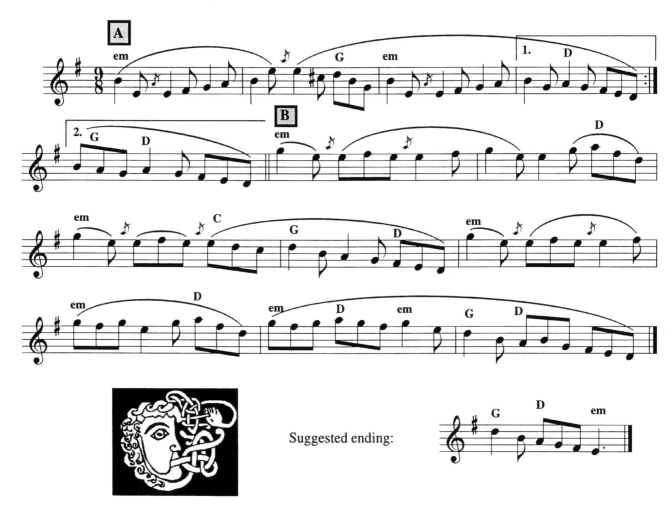

Suggested ending:

14

Hornpipe

The **hornpipe** is played at a slower tempo than the reel, and in a more heavily accented fashion.

It is customary for the closing bars of each section in a hornpipe to end with a ♩ ♩ ♩ rhythm.

The dotted eighth/sixteenth rhythm usually prevails in the performance of the hornpipe, although it is frequently notated as a pattern of straight eighth notes.

The hornpipe may also be distinguished by its formal structure. While it is often in two-part (AB) form, extended forms (ABC, ABCD, AABA, etc.) may differentiate it from the reel.

Cronin's Rambles

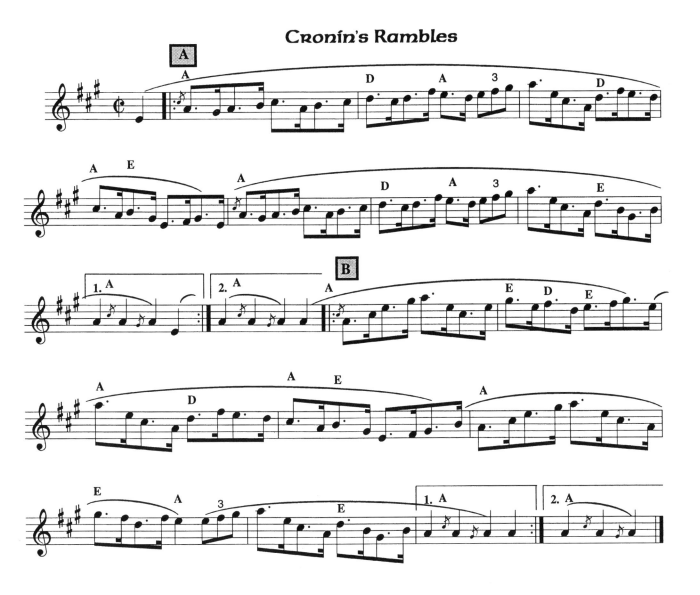

Reel

The **reel** is the most popular genre of tunes played by traditional instrumentalists. It is often played at a fast tempo, consequently it appeals to the virtuoso player. Strings of repeated eighth notes are associated with the reel.

Performance practice allows the substitution of dotted

or triplet figures, although the reel is traditionally notated with even eighth notes as in the following example:

The Flower of the Flock

Set Dance

Set dances were usually written for a particular dance. They are distinguished from other dance forms because the sections vary in length and/or time signature. The following set dance, for example, has an extended fourteen measure B section:

The Job of Journey Work

The Blackbird

(Set dance in duple meter with extended B section)

Performance Practice

Mere familiarity with the structural outline of an Irish tune does not allow the untrained player to render a tune satisfactorily. It is by understanding how stylistic elements are applied to Irish music that one can approximate a more traditional approach to playing. Listening to live and/or recorded performances, studying with traditional players, and working through written methods for learning to play in the Irish style are all ways to gain an accurate understanding of performance practice.

Stylistic elements affecting traditional performance practice include: tempo, rhythm, phrasing, breath control, ornamentation, and the process of variation. A discussion of these elements and examples for study and practice follow.

Tempo

The tempo (speed of performance) of a piece can vary due to the mood and skill of the performer. When learning to play a tune, it is best to practice at a slower tempo if note accuracy is of concern. It must be remembered that selection of a tempo is flexible, and that it can alter the character of a tune completely. A reel when played extremely fast can be a solo artist's tour de force, yet it might be unsuitable for those trying to dance a reel to the music. The player must decide for himself which tempo best fits the character and use of the piece. Listening to recorded versions of the same piece by different artists will give one a better idea of how tempo can vary within acceptable limits.

Rhythm

In written sources of traditional Irish music, tunes are most often presented with very little ornamentation or rhythmic alteration. As the previous discussion of Irish music indicated it is common to vary notated rhythms. In common (C) or cut time ($\cent$), running eighth notes

In compound times ($\frac{6}{8}$, $\frac{9}{8}$, $\frac{12}{8}$) a pattern of three eighth notes may be interpreted as The player should note that rhythmic variation is not employed by all players, nor is it used all of the time by any one player. It is up to the performer to decide which type of variation (if any) will enhance the rhythmic flow of the tune.

Phrasing

A phrase marking in music is similar to a sentence in prose. It indicates a complete musical thought and is used to give structure and continuity to the performance of a piece.

Written sources of traditional music do not include phrase markings because they can vary widely, and their placement contributes to the unique stylistic interpretation of a tune. As a general rule, the symmetrical construction of most dance tunes (two eight bar sections) allows a regular break in phrasing to occur every two or four measures as in the following example:

Take Your Choice

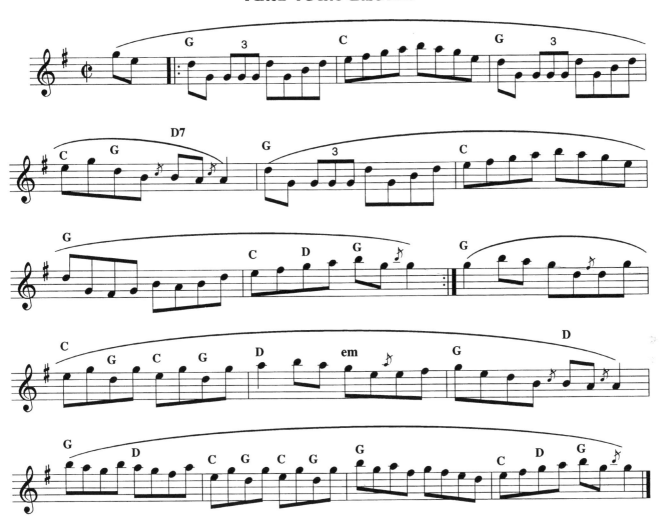

Phrasing is not always confined by the bar line, and the skillful musician will use the phrase to place emphasis on certain notes or to add rhythmic interest to a tune. Notes at the end of one phrase, for example, may be used as pick-up notes to the next phrase. This type of "phrasing across the bar line" is a common characteristic of traditional performance practice. It is shown in *Your Mother's Fair Pet.*

21

Your Mother's Fair Pet

Common indicators for appropriate phrase markings may also be observed
in the above example. Notes of longer duration towards the end of a measure
often serve as phrase endings and/or places to take a breath. The contour (shape) of
the musical line may also indicate a logical point at which to end or begin a phrase.
In the above example a large leap after a line of descending notes indicates the
ending point of one phrase and the beginning of a new phrase. In any case the
phrasing should assist the performer in playing with expression and cause little
interruption in the flow of the musical line. More often than not the traditional
player has an approach to phrasing where the rule is "Keep the music flowing
and take a breath when you need it—the rest will take care of itself."

Breath Support

In the classical sense, the term breath support describes control of the air stream through use of the diaphragm. Traditional players gain control of this musculature by repeated and forceful playing of long phrase lines. The use of breath support to taper phrasing in the classical sense is not customarily applied in the folk tradition. At the end of a long phrase the formally trained player will tend to support the pitch, and taper the envelope and volume of the sound.

The folk player will very often end a lively phrase with an accentuated push of air from the diaphragm. This is either followed by a natural decay of sound or a cutting off of the sound with a glottal stop (stopping air with the throat).

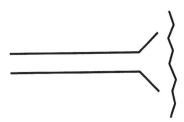

In slow airs the reverse situation is sometimes applied. A phrase ending or the last note of a piece may drop off in both pitch and volume. This practice adds character and style to the performance of a work. If such a technique is used by the classically trained player it would be notated deliberately for use in a contemporary work.

Control of the air stream may also be used by the folk player to imitate the shuffling sound/rhythm of a fiddle

String players control their sound with pressure of the bow arm and wind players must exercise control of the air stream to create bowing effects.

A thrust of air from the diaphragm is used by some traditional players to accentuate the rhythmic pulse of a tune. For example, the meter of a dance tune can be stressed by pulsating every other beat in a reel, or every beat in a jig. This may be a timing device for the musician (similar to beating the foot), but it establishes a rhythmic lilt that is associated with traditional performance practice. Pulsations may be practiced in an exaggerated fashion at first until the player feels comfortable with the technique. Judicious use of the breath as an ornament is recommended until the player is able to add pulsations without detracting from the performance of a dance tune. Accents are placed in the hornpipe *Tim the Turncoat* to show the player where pulsations would occur with this type of rhythmic enhancement.

Tim the Turncoat

Ornamentation

Slide

The **slide** is used to give emphasis to a note or phrase, and it is performed by gradually sliding the finger off of a tone hole. The slide occurs between two adjacent notes, and it is performed by the finger positioned over the lowest covered tone hole. For example:

Finger the note G and gradually slide the third finger of the left hand off of the tone hole until the note A sounds.

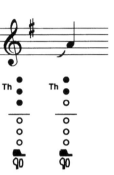

There is not a standard notational symbol for the slide, however, the symbol shown above will be used to indicate a slide in the remaining portion of this text.

On the French open-hole flute the notes on which a slide can be employed in this manner are limited. Try those on the following chart:

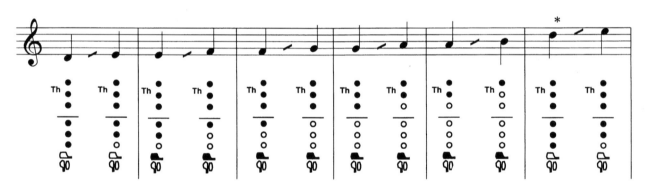

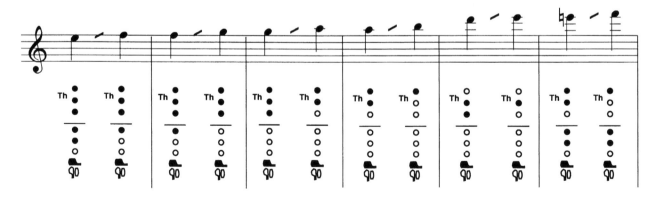

*The first finger must remain down for this slide to sound.

By sliding the finger half-way off of the tone hole onto the rim of the key, additional slides may be performed. The ⊖ symbol is used to indicate the covering of a key-rim only.

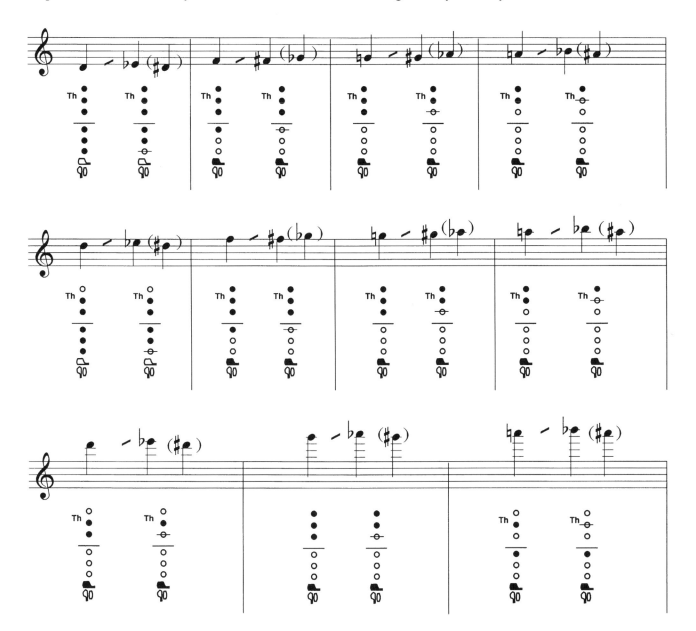

Note: The combination of this method of sliding with the alternative method listed below may be necessary for smooth transition from one note to the next.

Alternative Method for Sliding

The effect of a slide can also be produced by starting a note with the flute rotated inwards with maximum coverage of the embouchure hole. A rapid turning out of the flute while lifting the head to expose more of the embouchure hole creates a pitch modulation and sliding effect. The sliding motion over keywork on Boehm flutes may cause the flute to need periodic adjustment to assure adequate closure of the key pads. It is for this reason that rolling the headjoint may be a preferred method of sliding. One advantage of this method is that any note throughout the range of the instrument may be affected, although it does require much control over hand position and embouchure.

Tunes for Practicing the Slide

To the Men at Sea

M.M./D.G.

Light from Ennistimon

M.M./D.G.

Cut

The **cut** is a grace note, or a note played quickly **before** the principal note. It is used to:

a) emphasize or accentuate a particular note, or

b) to separate two notes of the same pitch.

The term **cut** refers to a note **above** the principal note.* Cuts on simple system flutes are commonly performed on the notes **D, E, F#, G, A,** and **B**; however, cuts may be performed throughout the entire range of the Boehm flute. Numerous fingerings will produce cuts, and it is advisable to experiment in order to find the fingerings that will achieve the desired effect as well as facilitate ease in playing your instrument.

The sounding note of a cut is usually chosen for its pronounced, clean, and noticeable delineation from the prinicipal note. It is also chosen for ease of fingering. The simple system player has a limited and manageable number of fingering options for sounding cuts. The Boehm flutist, on the other hand, is presented with a large number of choices with which to maneuver cut fingerings and the options may at first seem overwhelming. Some players may wish to simplify their approach to playing cuts by following 'the road of least resistance.' For example, when a cut works for multiple fingerings, then use only that cut fingering. This approach does not always take key signature into consideration, but it is a quick way of getting started.

A simplified fingering chart for cuts on Boehm flutes follows along with tunes for practicing the cut. The fingerings given in the tunes for practice allow the player to maneuver cuts without slowing down to learn all of the available fingering options. A more detailed cut fingering chart is found on pages 180-183. If a given fingering does not work well on your instrument then consult the detailed chart as it may provide a more suitable alternative for your instrument.

*A grace note **below** the principal note is called a **tip** or **strike**.

The tip is used most frequently in the context of a long or short roll (see section discussing these ornaments). The tip may also be used to separate two notes of the same pitch. In these instances the tip is fingered with standard fingerings.

Cuts

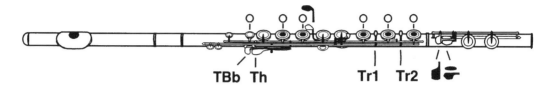

TBb Th   Tr1 Tr2

This chart shows **selected** cut fingerings for the French open-hole flute. A great number of alternate fingerings are not shown here. See pages 180-183 for a more comprehensive chart.

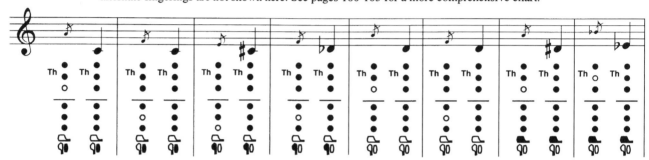

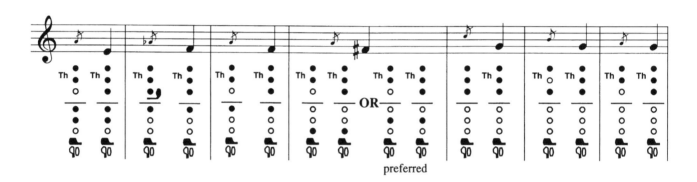

preferred

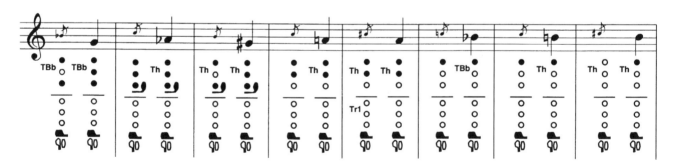

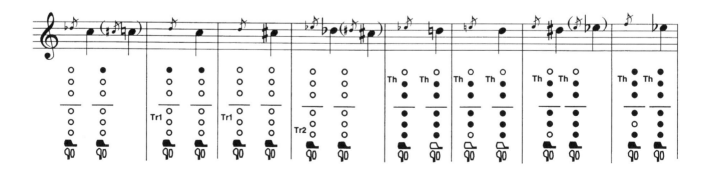

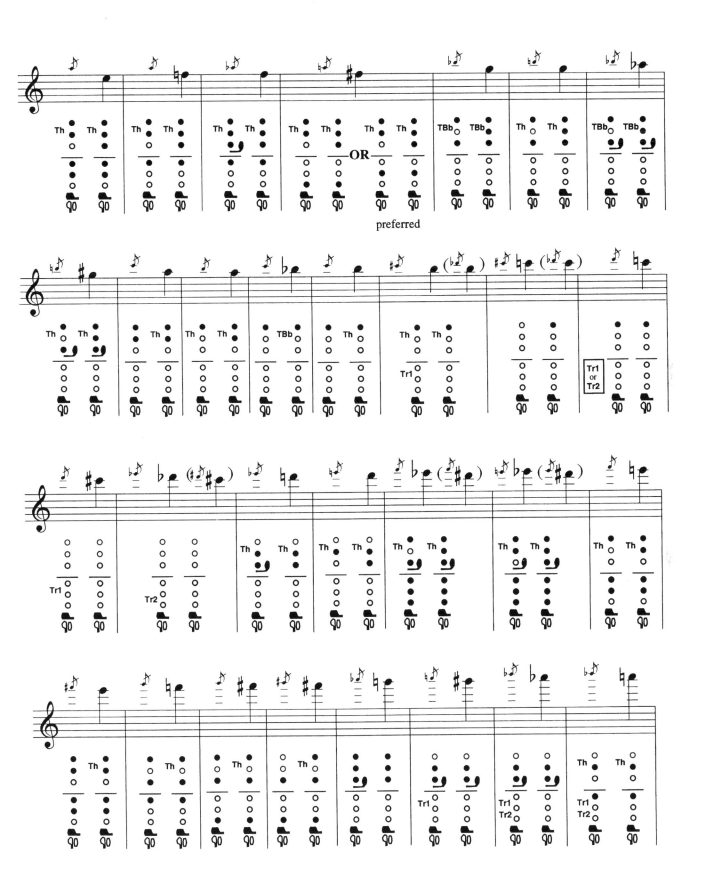

preferred

31

Cuts Between Two Notes of the Same Pitch

When the cut is used to separate two notes of the same pitch it is not necessary to rearticulate (tongue) the cut. It is played under one breath.

Scale Practice

Scales for practicing cuts between two notes of the same pitch follow. The entire gamut of keys is not represented here. Keys of up to four sharps and four flats are presented in this book as a practical means of expanding the normal parameters of tonality used in the Irish folk tradition. Cuts in the following scale patterns retain the attributes (sharps and flats) of their key signatures. The player may also wish to use cut fingerings that fall outside of the given keys. Check pages 180-183 for alternate cut fingerings.

C Major

D Major

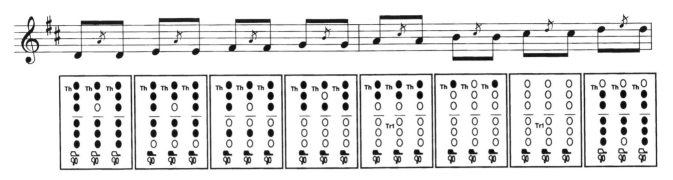

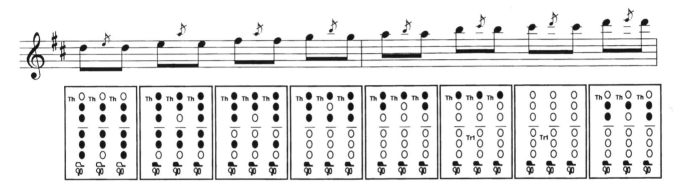

E Flat Major

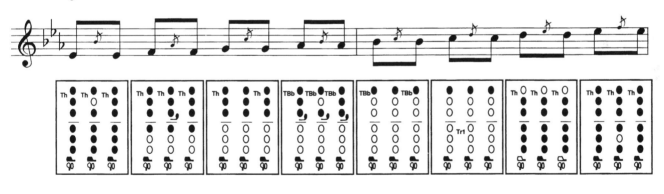

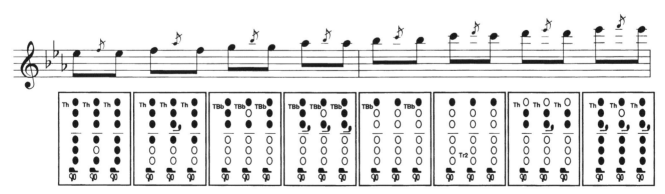

33

E Major

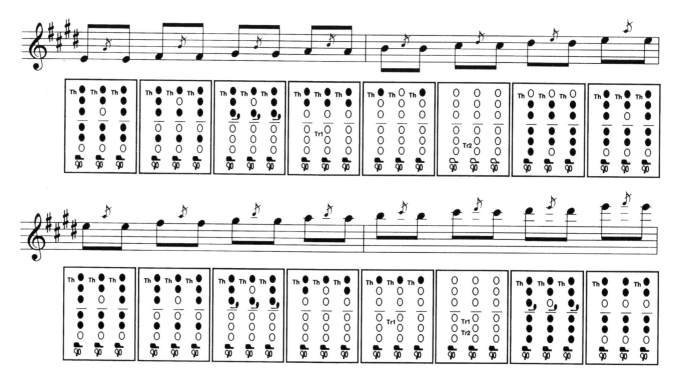

F Major

34

G Major

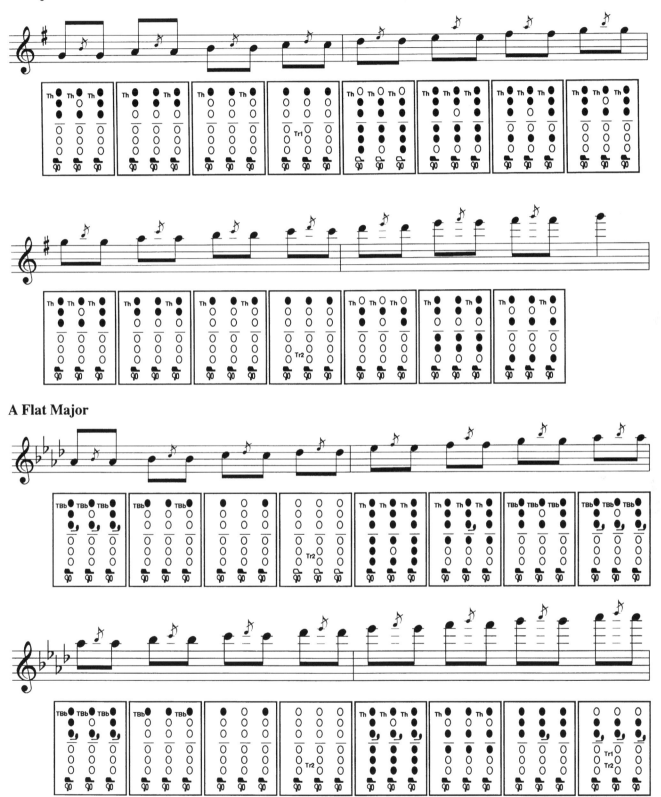

A Flat Major

A Major

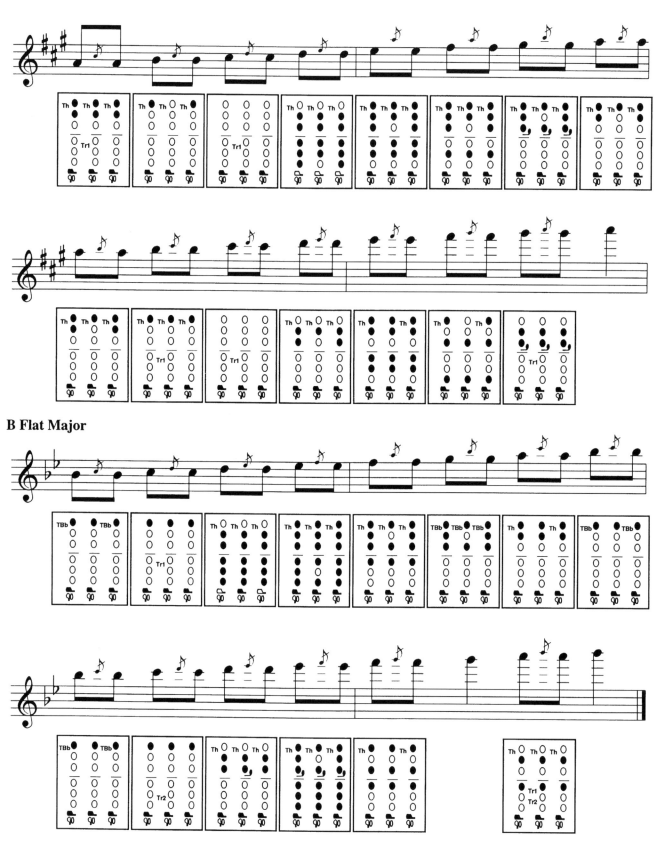

B Flat Major

36

Tipperary Hills

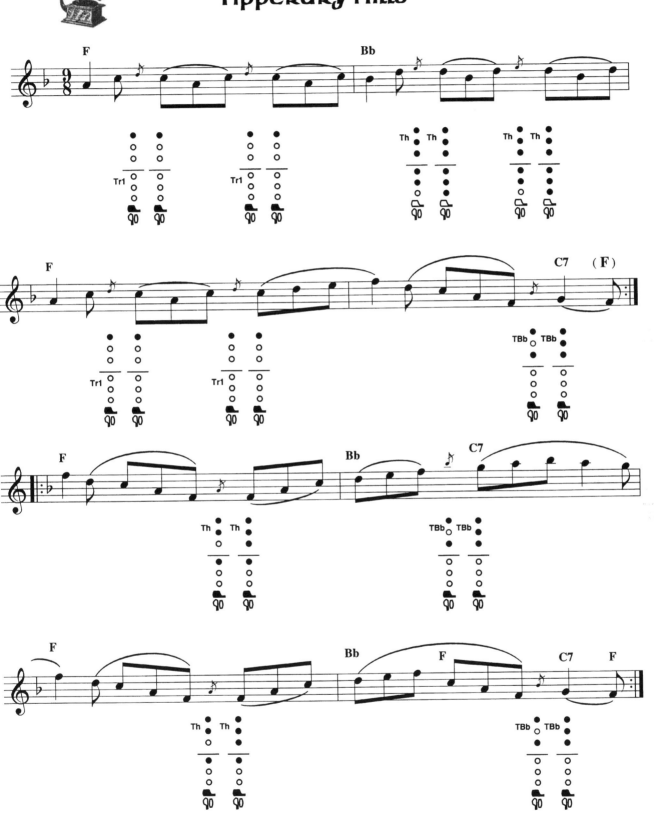

The Bloom of Youth

Come Along With Me

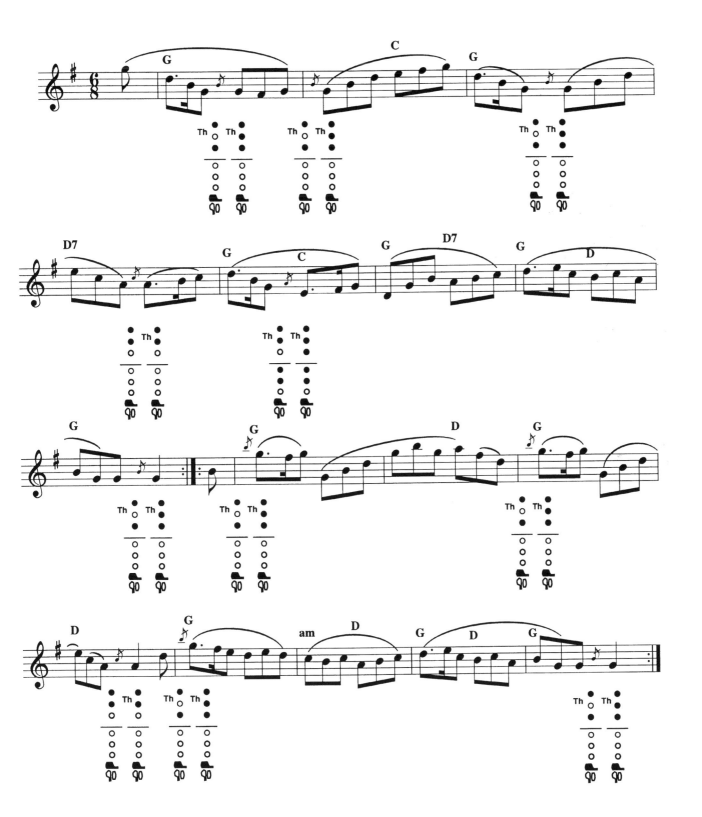

Galway Tom

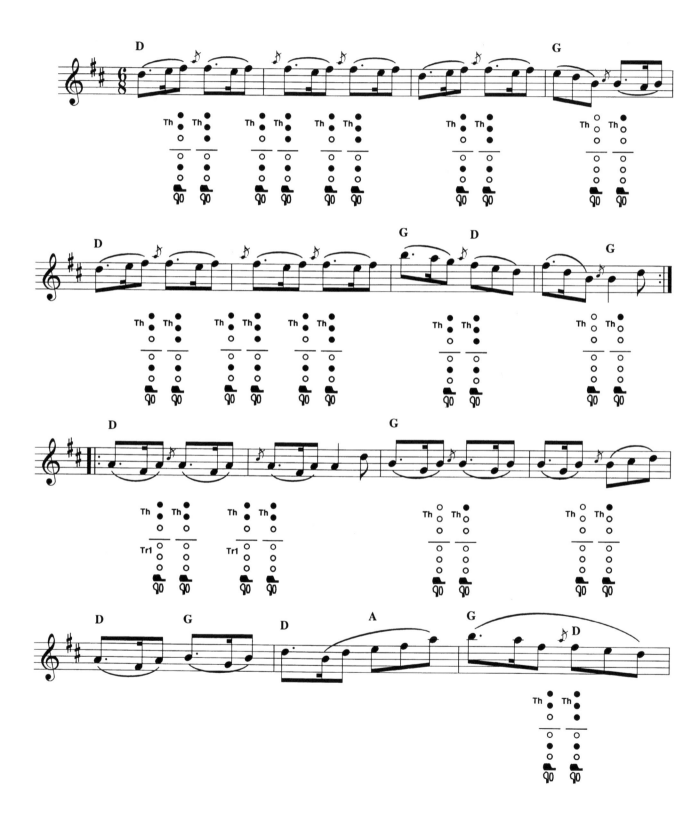

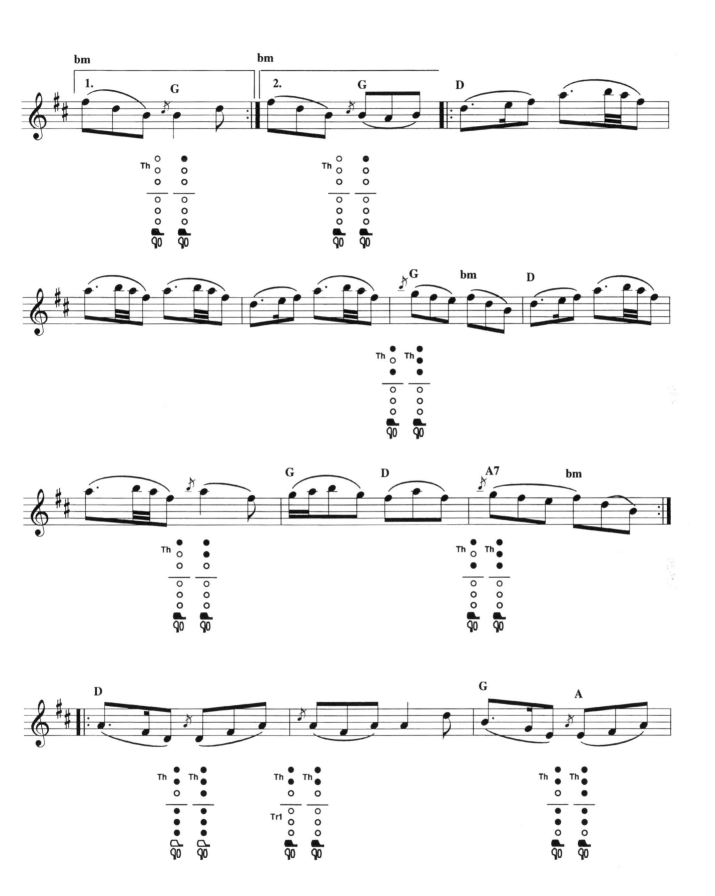

41

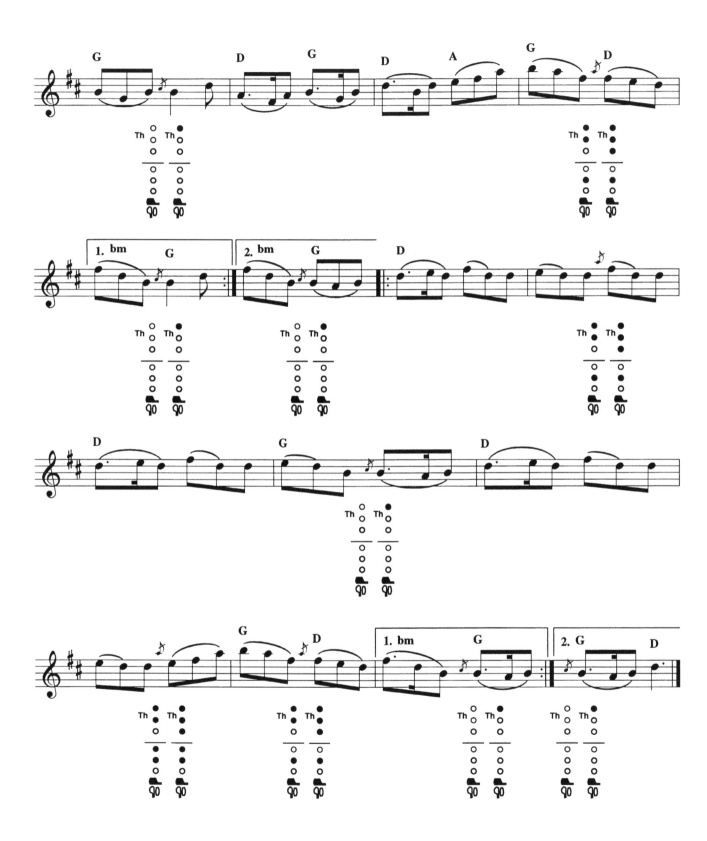

The Happy Days of Youth

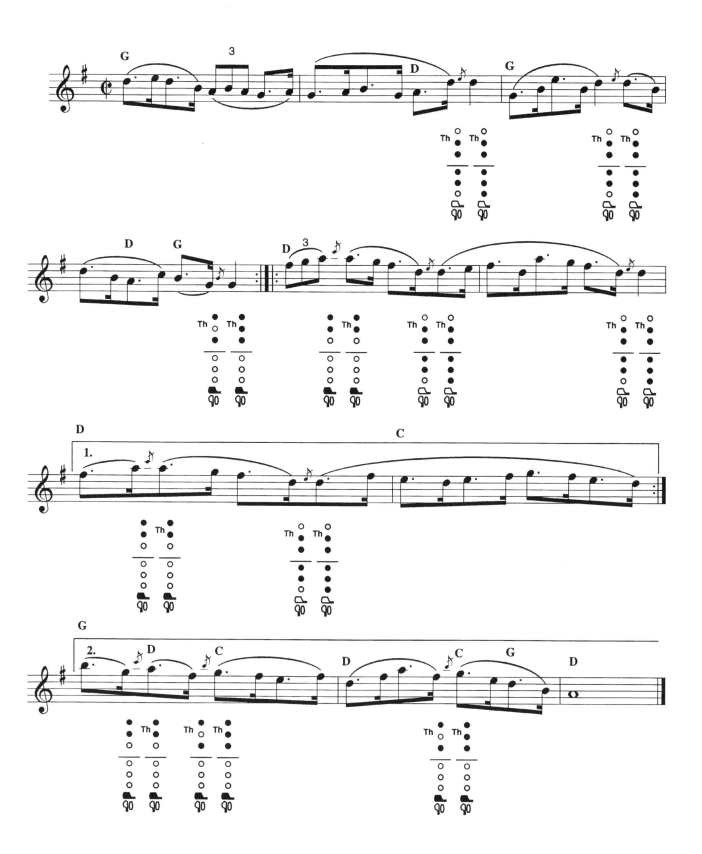

Johnny's Wedding

Wellington's Advance

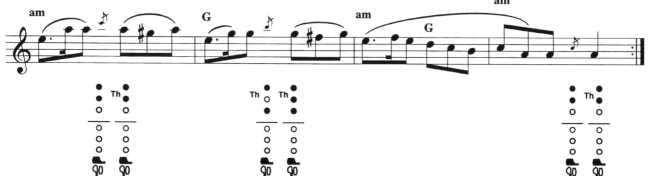

The Jolly Corkonian

Double Grace Notes

Double grace notes are similar to cuts between two notes of the same pitch except that the initial principal note is part of the ornament. Grace notes are played quickly before the entrance of the principal note. As with cuts, many alternate fingerings may be used when executing this ornament. Consult the detailed fingering chart for cuts on pages 180-183.

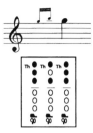

Another type of double grace ornament is familiar to classically trained musicians. It is formed by the principal note and its upper neighbor tone (scale tone directly above the principal note). It may be substituted for the double grace figure described above. Standard fingerings and trill fingerings are used in the execution of this ornament. Consult pages 184-186 for a chart of trill fingerings.

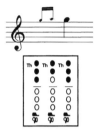

A less common double grace figure is formed by tipping the principal note (playing the scale tone directly below the principal note). Standard fingerings or trill fingerings are used in the execution of this ornament.

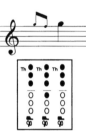

Scale Practice for Double Grace Notes

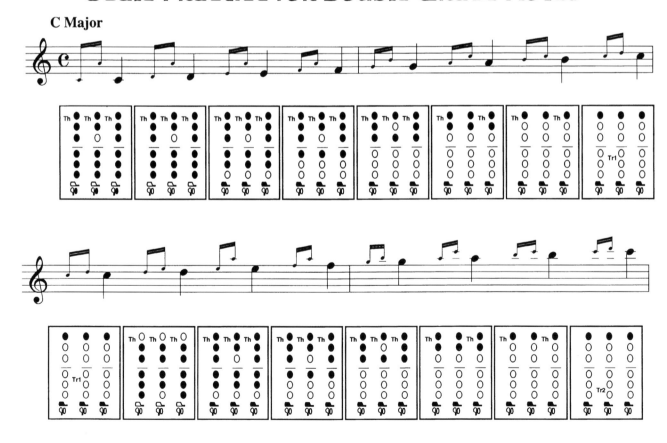

48

D Major

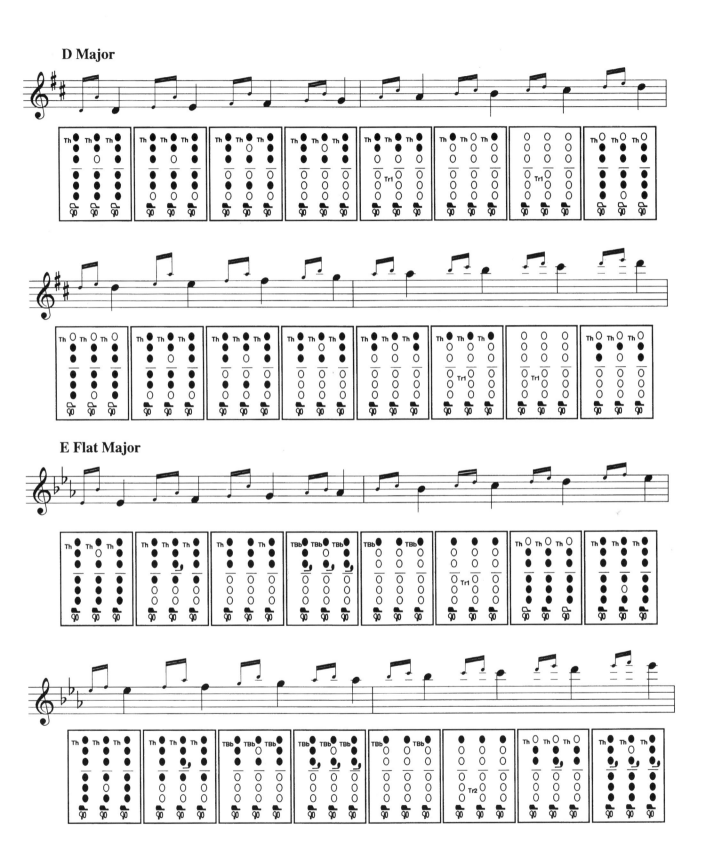

E Flat Major

E Major

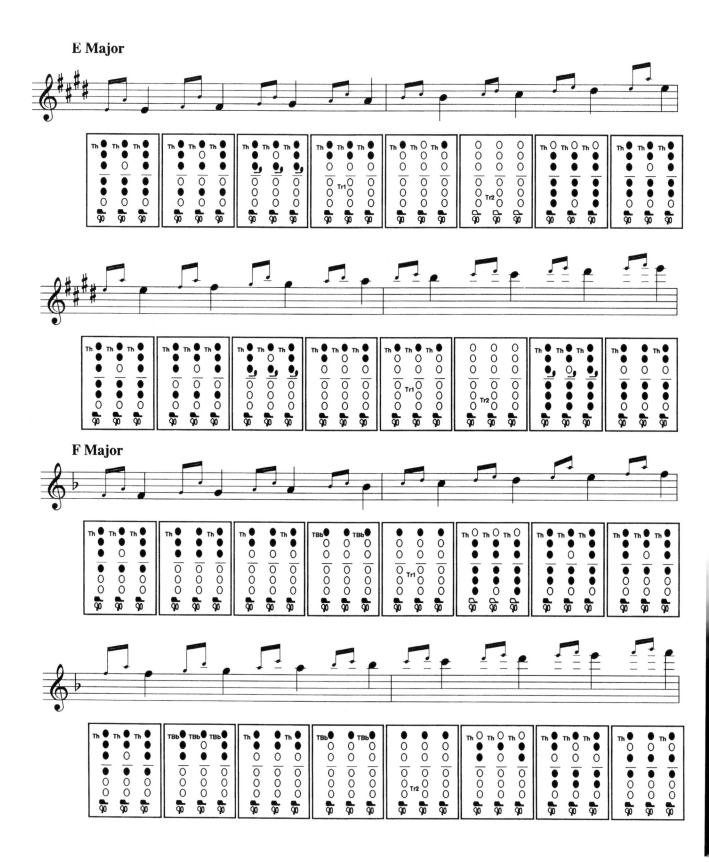

F Major

G Major

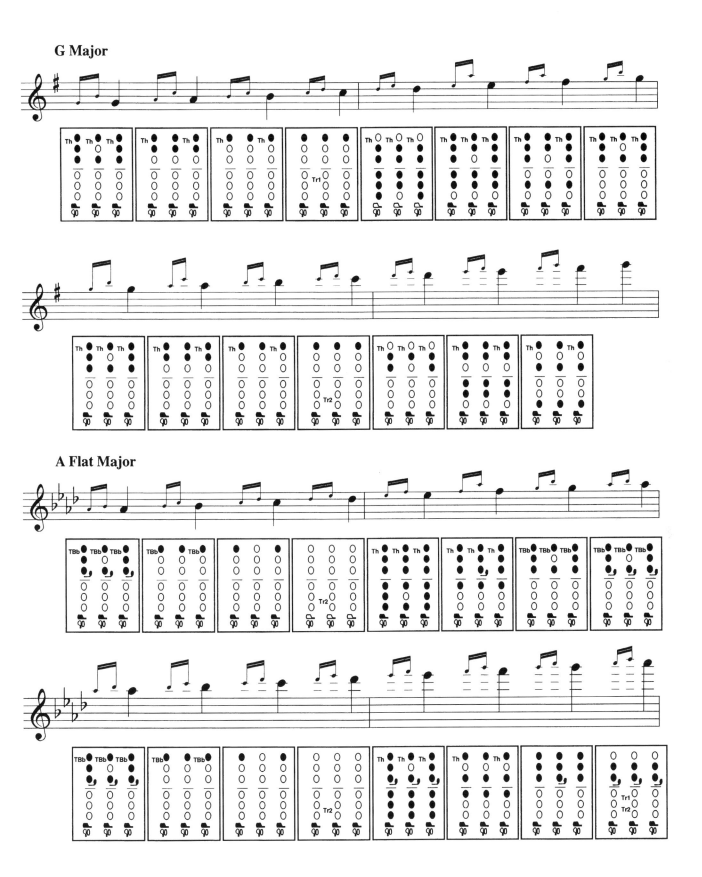

A Flat Major

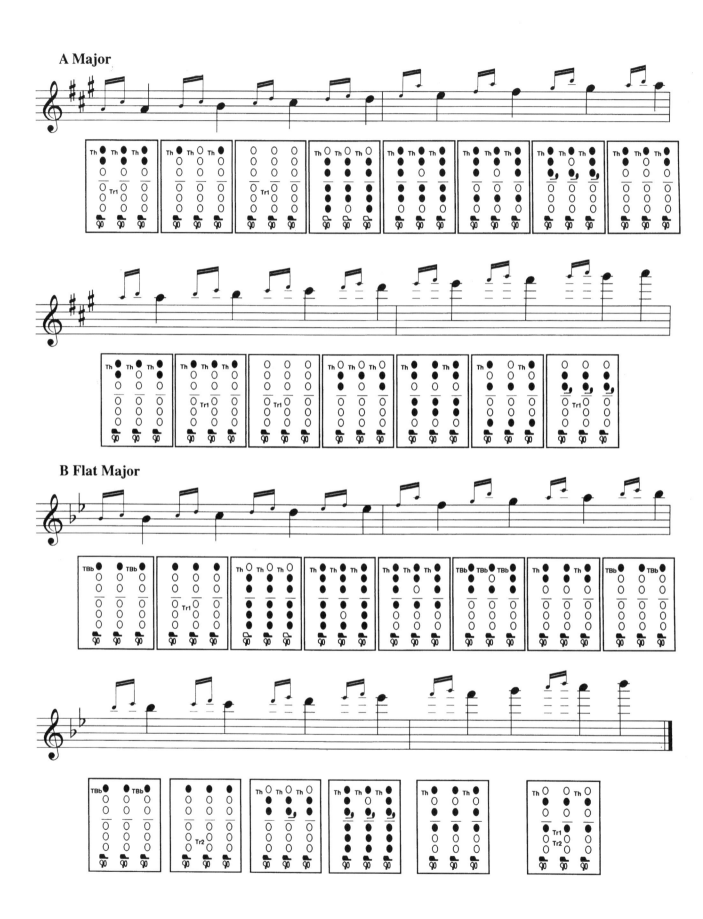

Julia McMahon

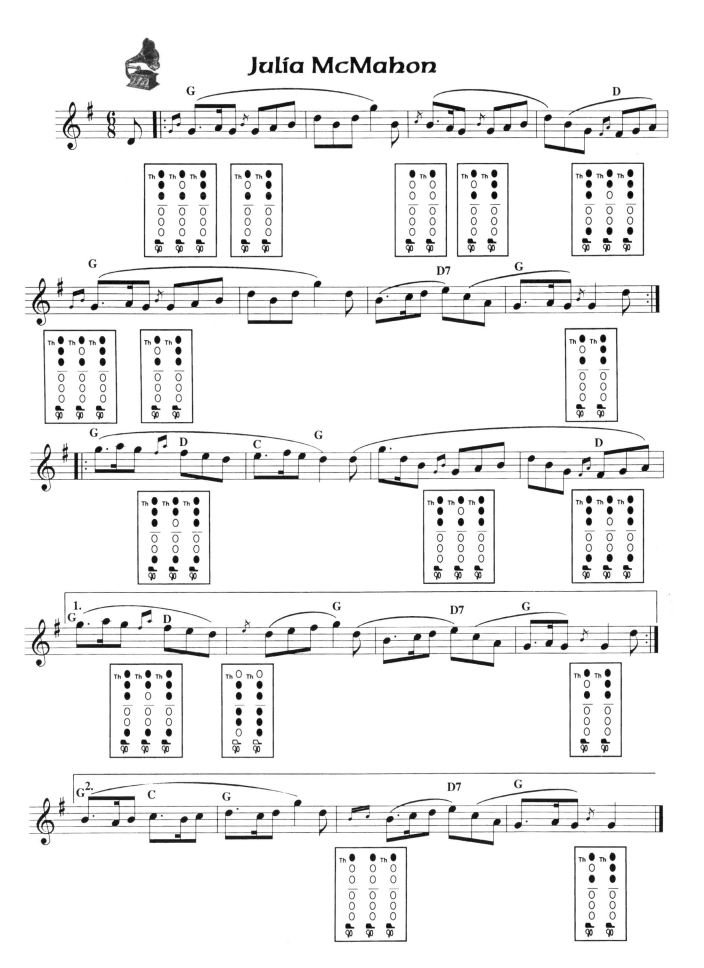

The Lovely Lad

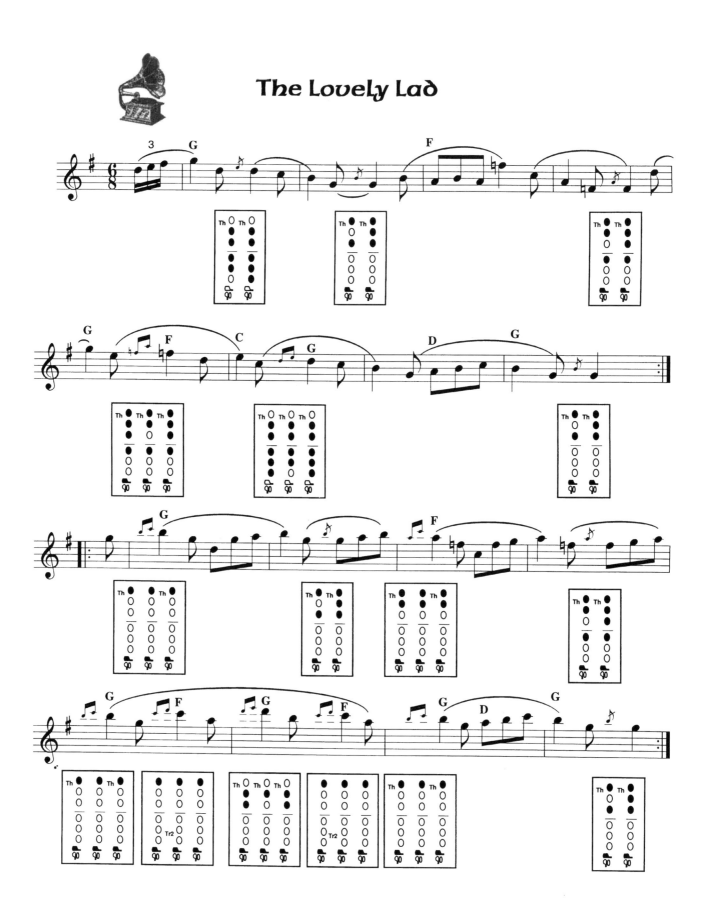

The Magpie's Nest

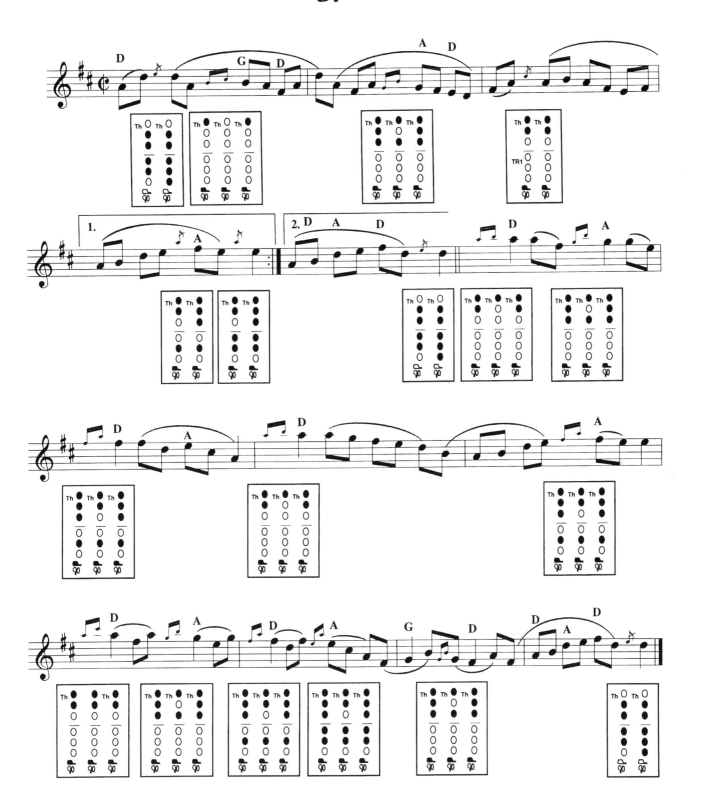

The Western Lasses

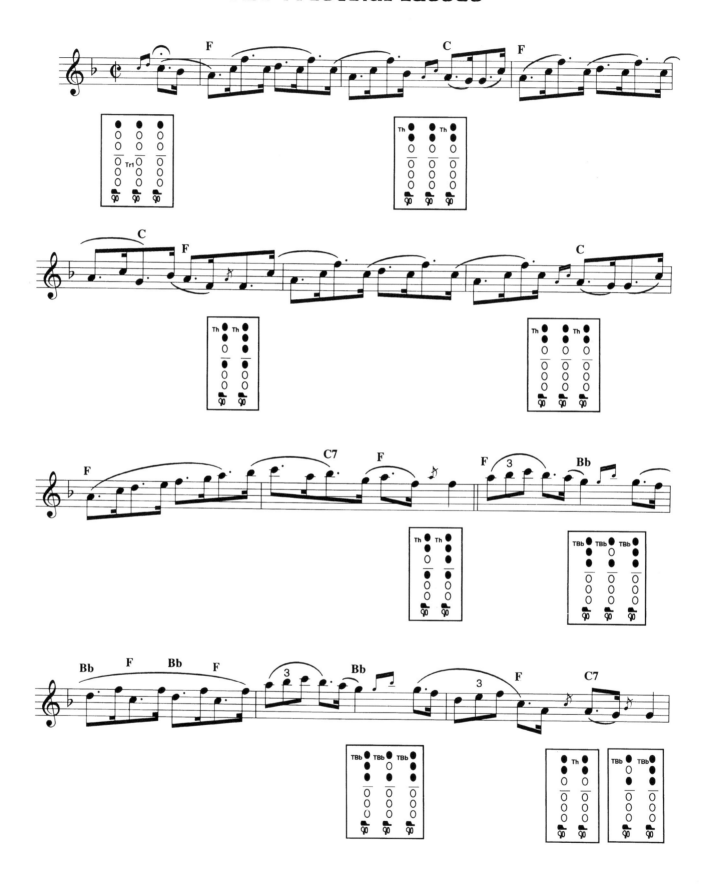

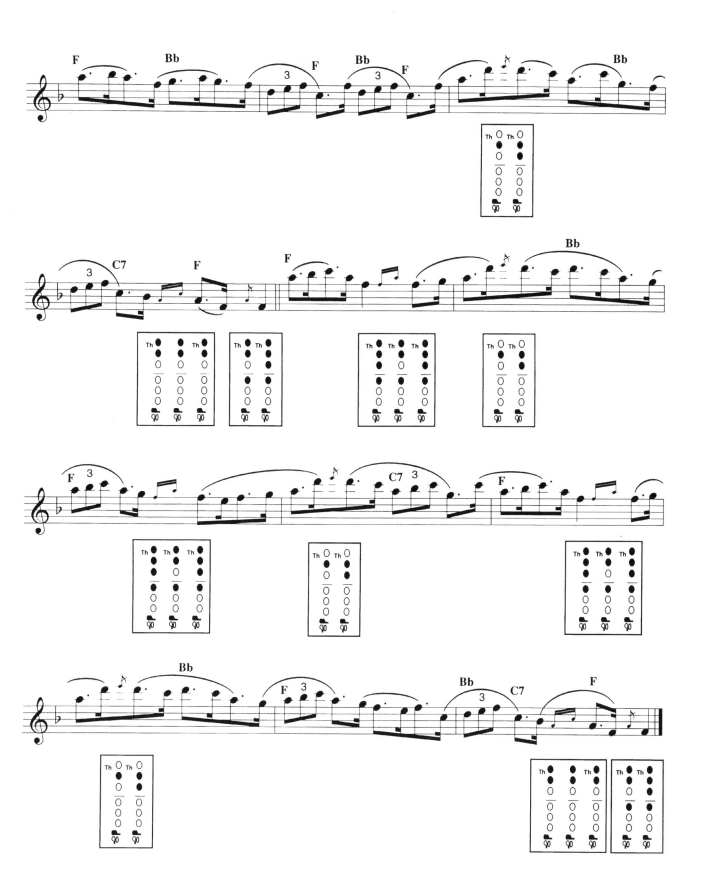

Leaves of Three

M.M./D.G.

58

The Rose in the Garden

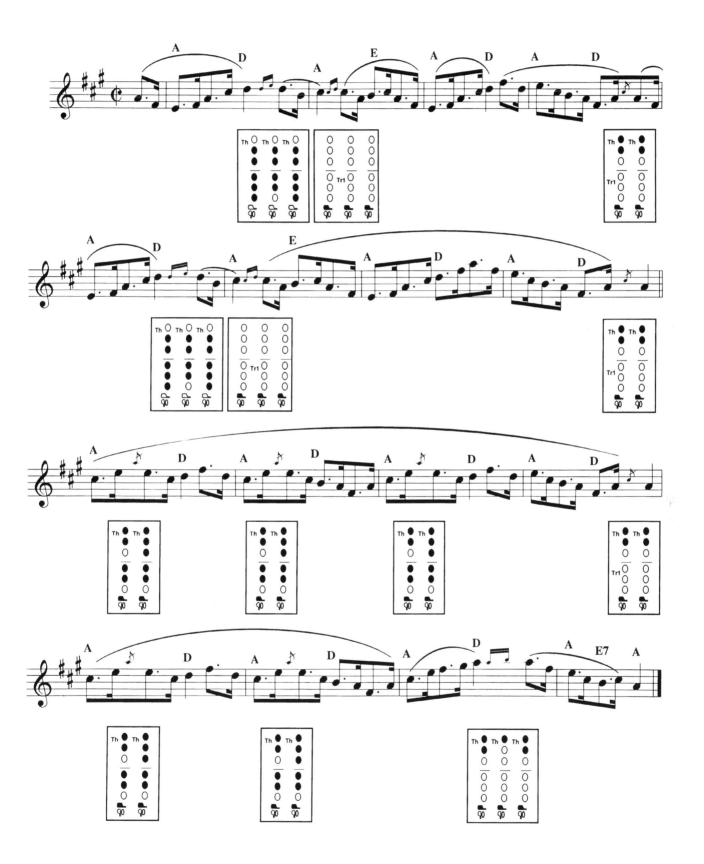

Triple Grace Notes

The **triple grace note** ornament is used infrequently, however, it may be added where a variety of ornamentation is desired. Triple grace notes consist of three short notes played quickly **before** the principal note. There are two types of triple grace notes:

1) The first type is familiar to classically trained players, and it consists of an upper neighbor tone, the principal note, and an upper neighbor tone.

Example:

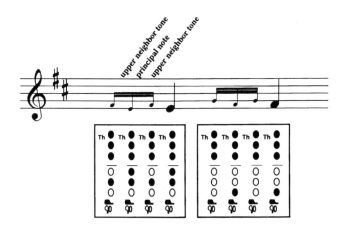

2) The second type stems from ornamentation used by pipers. It consists of a cut above the principal note, the principal note, and another **different** cut above the principal note. A variety of cuts and fingerings may be used in the construction of this ornament. Consult the extensive cut fingering chart on pages 180-183 when considering alternatives.

Example:

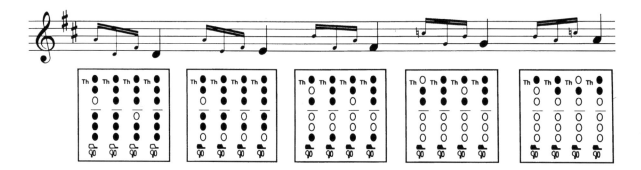

Note: The upper cuts can also be placed in ascending order as seen in the example above on the note A.

Jack of All Trades

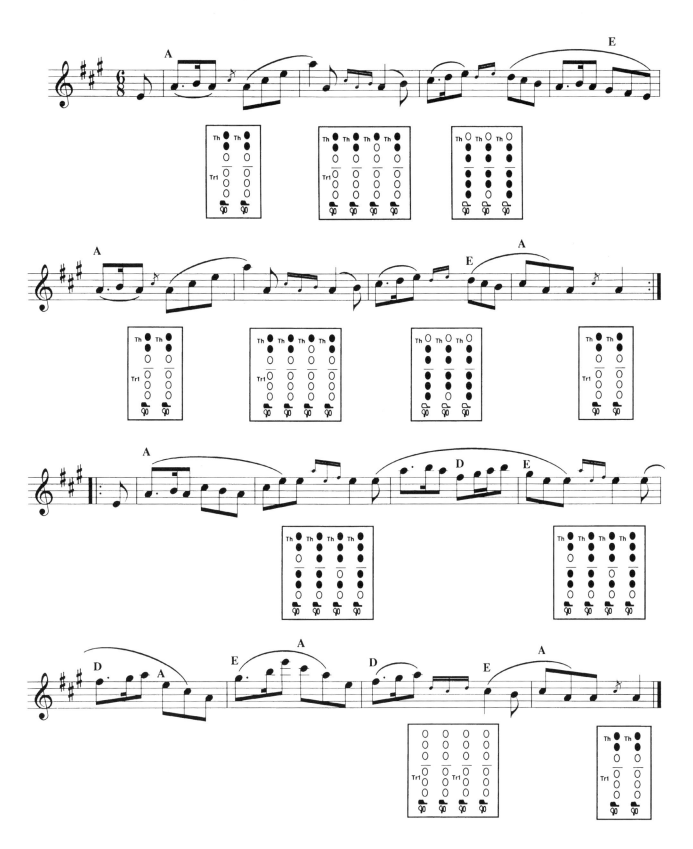

Triplets

A **triplet** is a group of three notes played in the time of two notes of the same value.
It is usually indicated by the number three placed above or below the group of three notes.

Example:

Triplets are used to:
1) Link notes separated by the interval of a third by filling in a passing tone.

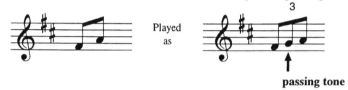

2) To add motion to a longer note by:
      a. Playing the principal note, its upper neighbor tone,
        and the principal note.

      b. Playing a group of three staccato (tongued/detached) notes on the same pitch.

3) To transcend smoothly an ascending or descending musical line.
   Notes are filled in or repeated as in the following examples:

Staccato Triplets

When the performance tempo is fast, the player may have difficulty quickly tonguing each note of a staccato triplet. A multiple articulation pattern may be used in faster passages to substitute for single strokes of the tongue. This involves the use of unvoiced syllables. Select a group of syllables that best approximates a clearly articulated triplet.

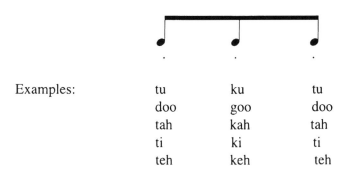

Examples:

tu	ku	tu
doo	goo	doo
tah	kah	tah
ti	ki	ti
teh	keh	teh

Although this may be cumbersome at first, careful practice that emphasizes evenness of all syllables will allow fast passages to be played with ease.

Dick Sand's Hornpipe

Triplets

The placement of triplets in a piece can vary, and when triplets are added at different times in repeated sections of music they will contribute to the distinctive character of each version. Two versions of *Hick's Hornpipe* follow. Grey boxes indicate the presence of a triplet in the ornamented version.

Hick's Hornpipe

After playing through this example, experiment on your own with the placement of triplets.

Hick's Hornpipe

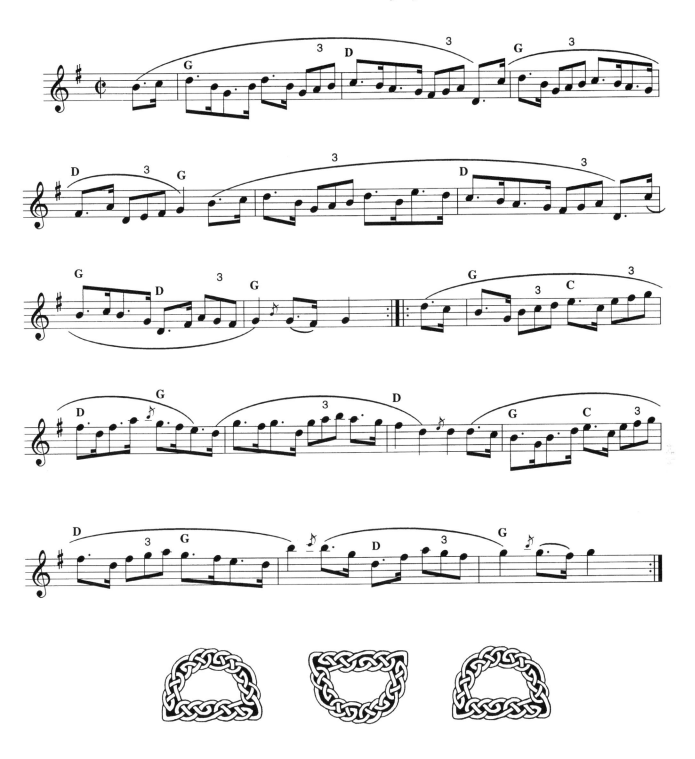

Fair and Forty

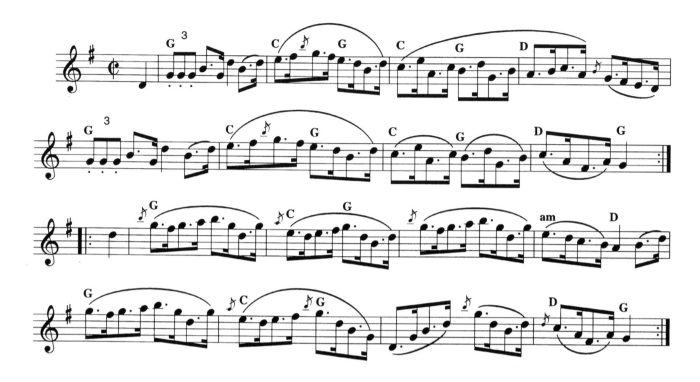

Early in the Morning

 # Rolls

The **roll** is an ornament that involves cutting and tipping a principal note. In each roll the principal note is ornamented with two grace notes: the first grace is above the principal note, and the second grace is below the principal note. The higher grace note is called a **cut**, and the lower grace note is called a **tip** or **strike**. The tip is usually the note directly below the principal note, and it retains the accidentals found in the key signature.

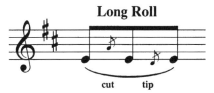

Short Roll

The short roll is used to ornament a quarter note or two eighth notes of the same pitch. It is performed and notated in a variety of ways:

1) As grace notes separating two eighth notes of the same pitch,

2) As triple grace notes,

3) As a triplet preceded by a grace note (sometimes called a graced triplet),

4) As four sixteenth notes,

Preferred Notation:

A ⌣ symbol (not to be confused with a fermata sign).

5) As a grace note preceding a dotted figure,

Short Roll Fingering Chart
(Selected Fingerings)

Major and minor key alterations are placed in the following chart for players who wish to maintain key attributes (sharps and flats) when performing this ornament. **Many other fingerings will work**, especially if the key attributes are not retained. Consult the detailed fingering chart on pages 180-183 for additional possibilities. **Experiment** with your instrument until you find a fingering pattern that suits your style and technique.

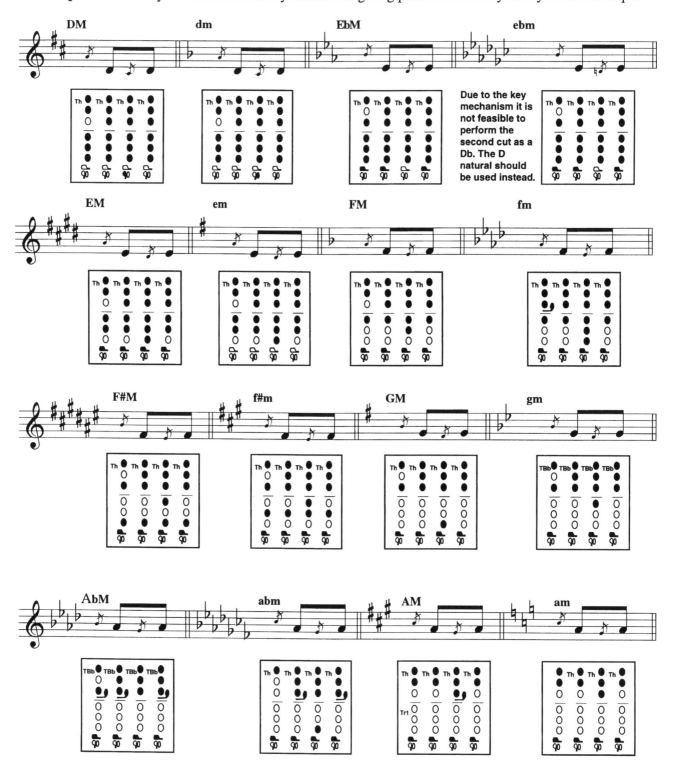

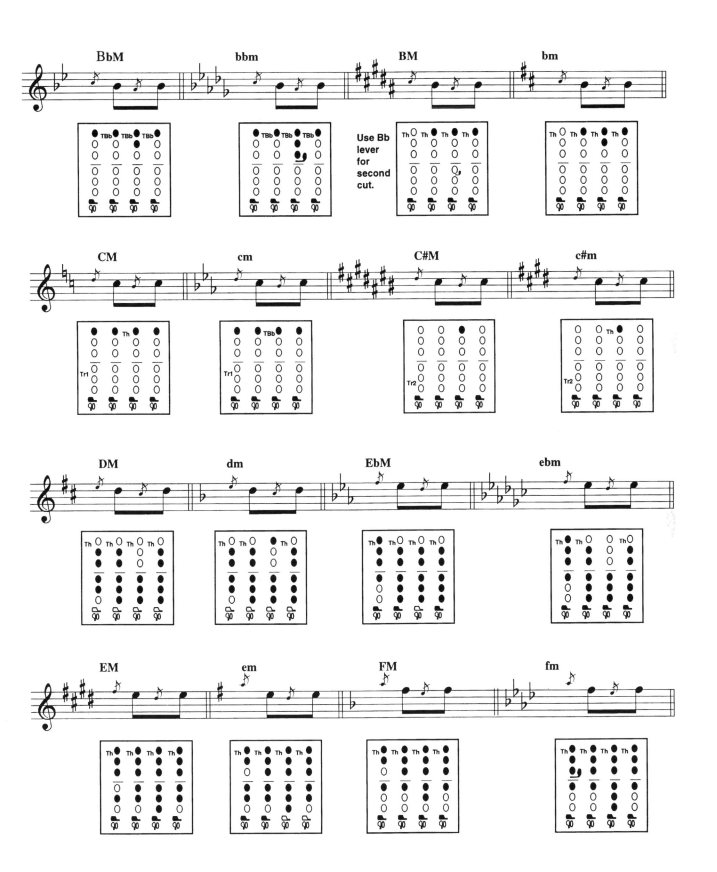

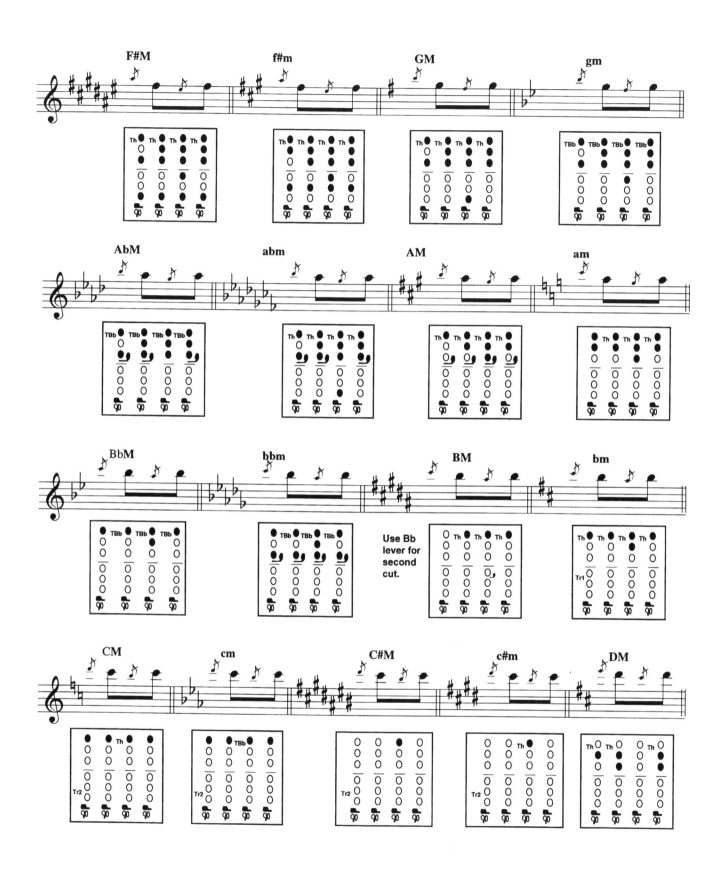

Note: It is possible to continue the range of rolled notes beyond high D.

The short roll can either add emphasis to a strong beat within a measure, or it can strengthen a weaker beat by giving it more motion. Two exercises follow for practicing the roll as it occurs in either position.

Major Key/Cyclical Short Roll Exercise/
Roll in Weak Position

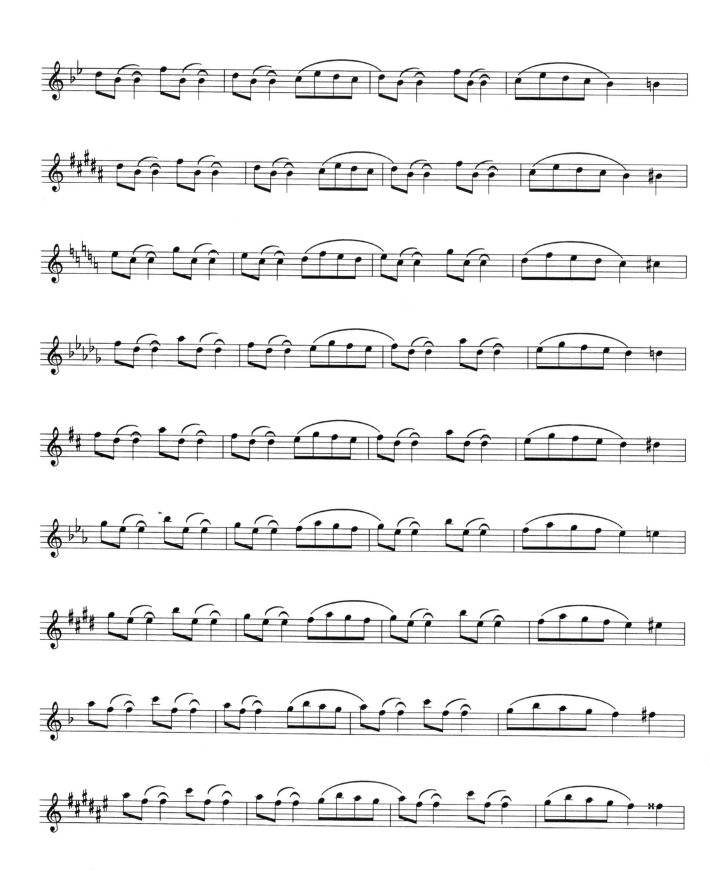

72

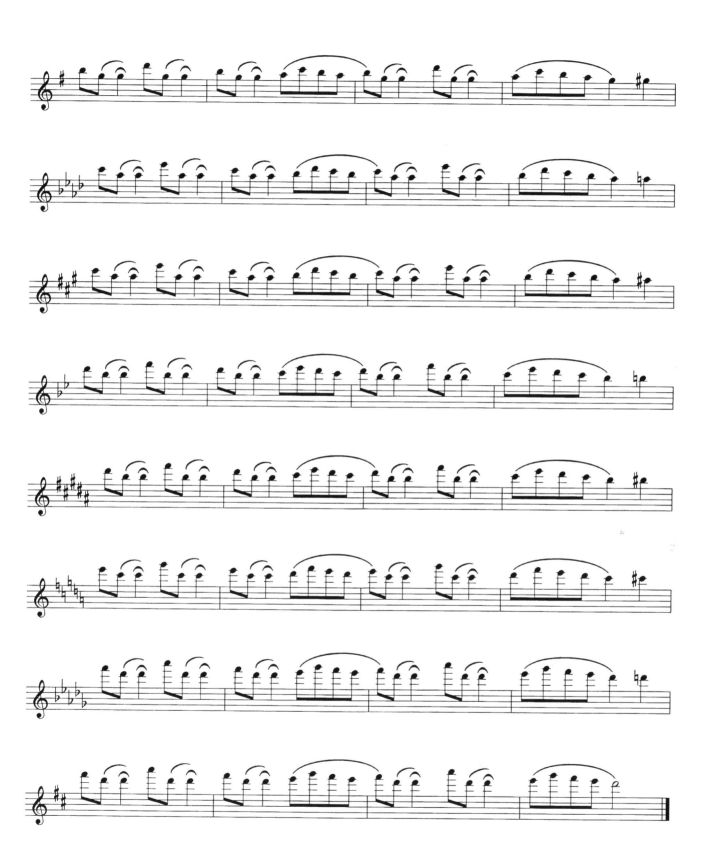

73

Major Key/Cyclical Short Roll Exercise/ Roll in Strong Position

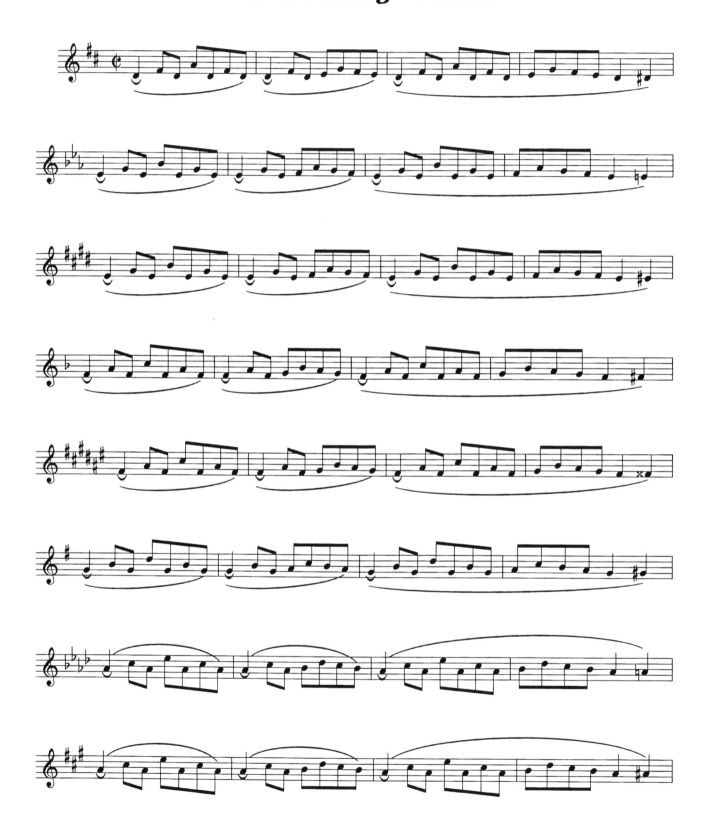

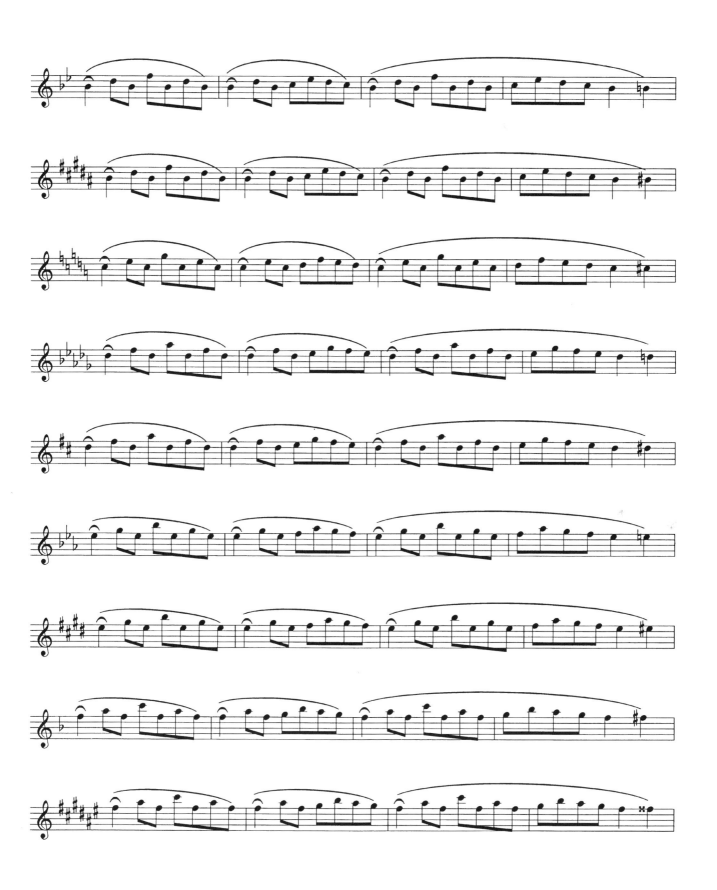

75

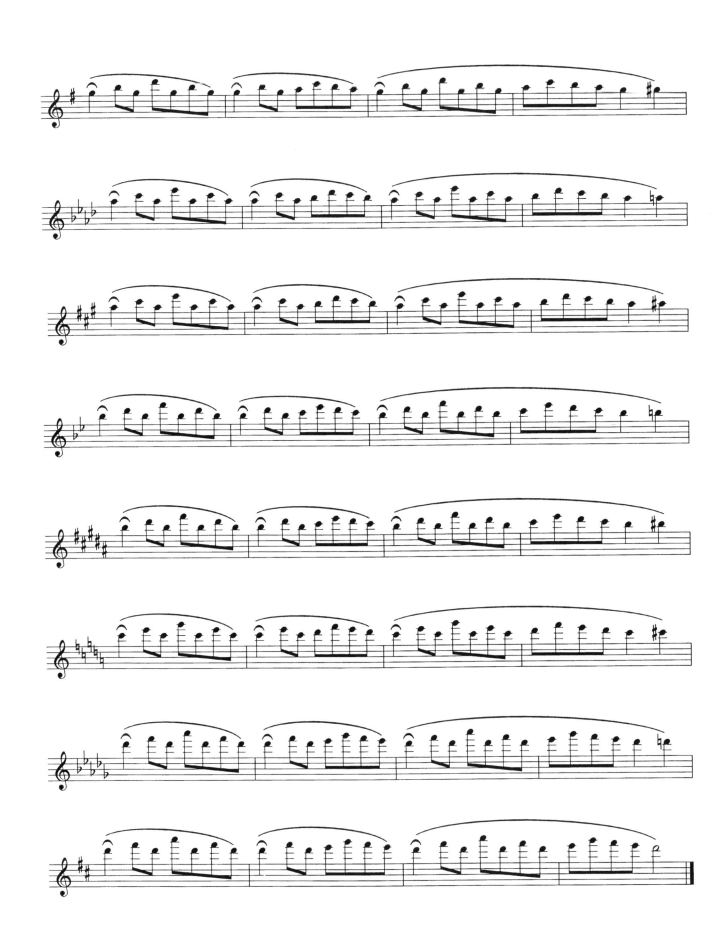

76

Short D Roll

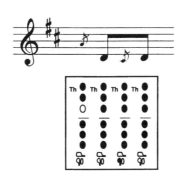

The Green Jacket

Short D Roll

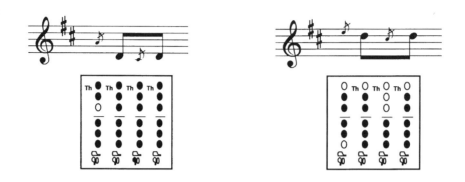

The Callan Lasses

Short E Roll

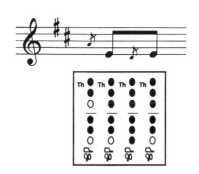

The Miltown Maid

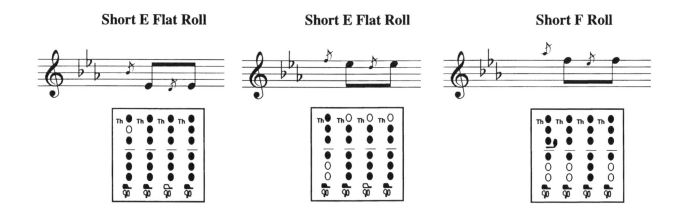

Short E Flat Roll　　　**Short E Flat Roll**　　　**Short F Roll**

Take Your Choice

Short F Roll

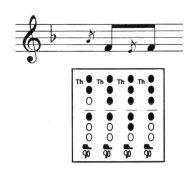

The Dublin Lasses

81

Short F Sharp Rolls

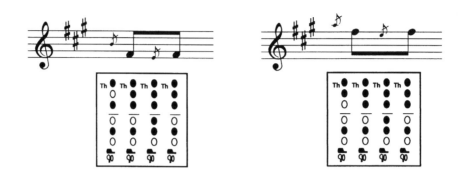

The Greenlefe Inn

M.M./D.G.

Short G Roll

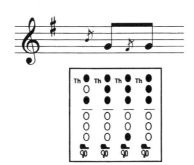

Touch Me If You Dare

Short A Flat Roll　　　　　　**Short E Flat Roll**

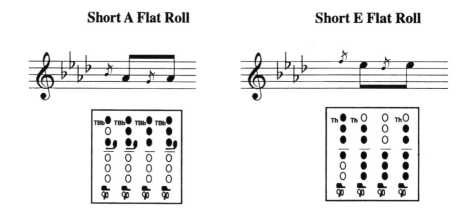

The Avonmore

Short A Roll

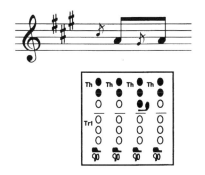

Humphrey's Hornpipe

Short A Roll

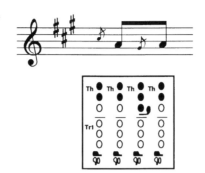

The Mason's Apron

Short B Flat Rolls

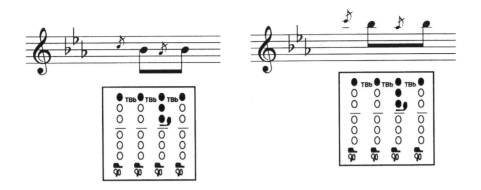

The Maid in the Cherry Tree

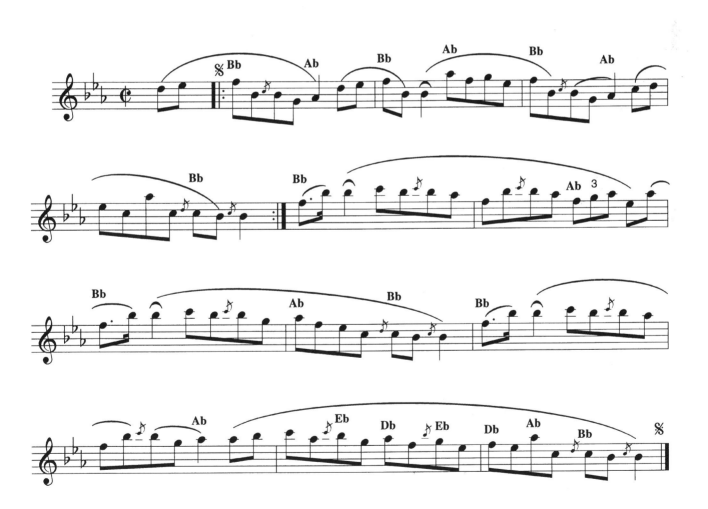

Short B Roll

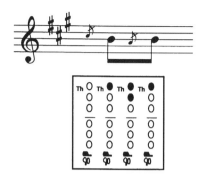

Peggy on the Settle

88

Short C Roll

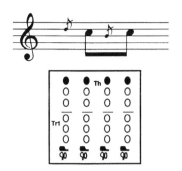

The Jolly Seven

Short C Sharp Roll

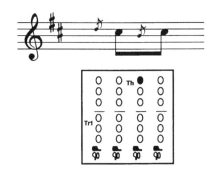

The New Demesne

Short A Roll   **Short E Roll**

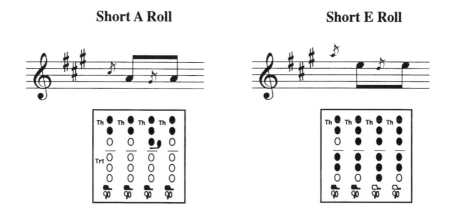

The Bloom of Youth

Short F Rolls

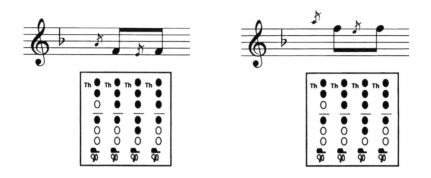

Captain Kelly's Reel

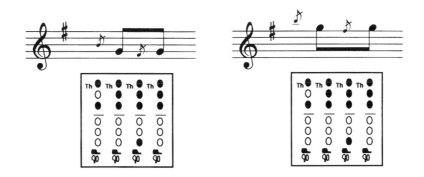

The Steam Packet

Short A Flat Roll   ### Short B Flat Roll   ### Short A Flat Roll

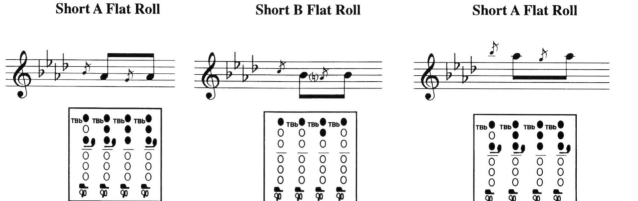

Note: Tip on A natural is preferred for this roll due to the ease of fingering.

Clancy's Fancy Reel

Short A Roll

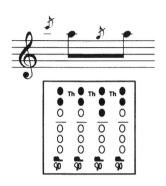

The Old Grey Gander

Short D Roll   Short E Flat Roll   Short B Flat Roll

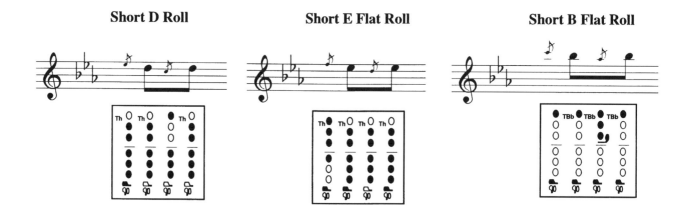

Coming Over the Hills

96

Short B Roll   **Short C Sharp Roll**

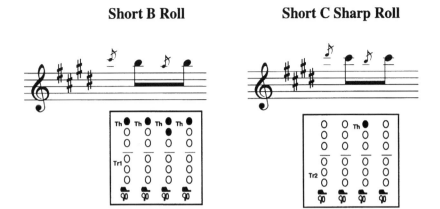

The Strawberry Blossom

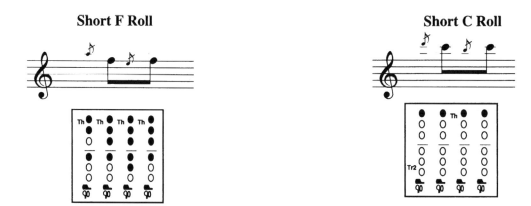

Short F Roll

Short C Roll

The Maíd at the Churn

Short C Roll

Short D Roll

The roll on high D is easier to perform when the tip remains a C# rather than a C natural.

O'Reilly's Greyhound

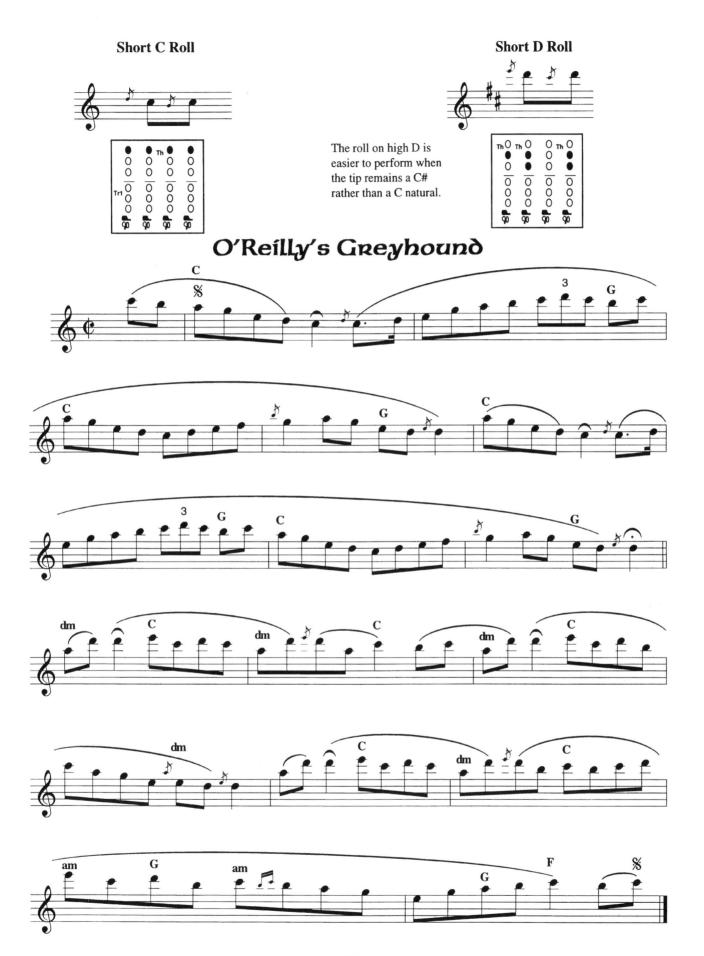

Long Roll

The long roll is used to ornament the dotted quarter note in both compound ($\frac{6}{8}$, $\frac{9}{8}$ etc.) and simple (¢ , $\frac{4}{4}$ etc.) time. Like the short roll, the long roll is performed and notated in a variety of ways:

1) As grace notes separating three notes of the same pitch.

   or

2) As a triplet placed between two notes of the same pitch.

3) As thirty-second notes following a long principal note.

4) As a gruppetto. The classically trained player will recognize the similarity of the long roll to the Baroque gruppetto. The gruppetto may be substituted for the long roll; however, it is not a preferred fingering since it uses an upper neighbor tone (note directly above the principal note) instead of a cut. The gruppetto figure uses standard fingerings throughout the range of the instrument.

5) As a quintuplet.

Preferred Notation:

A roll symbol.

The ⌣ or ⌢ symbol will be used to indicate a roll throughout the remaining portion of this text. A symbolic representation of the ornament encourages the player to rhythmically alter the roll to suit his/her taste. Listen to the performance of the rolls on the accompanying recording, and follow along in the music. You will soon acquire the ability to use the roll as a key element of ornamentation in the Irish style.

100

Long Roll Fingering Chart
(Selected Fingerings)

Major and minor key alterations are placed in the following chart for players who wish to maintain key attributes (sharps and flats) when performing this ornament. **Many other fingerings will work**, especially if the key attributes are not retained. Consult the detailed fingering chart on pages 180-183 for additional possibilities. **Experiment** with your instrument until you find a fingering pattern that suits your style and technique.

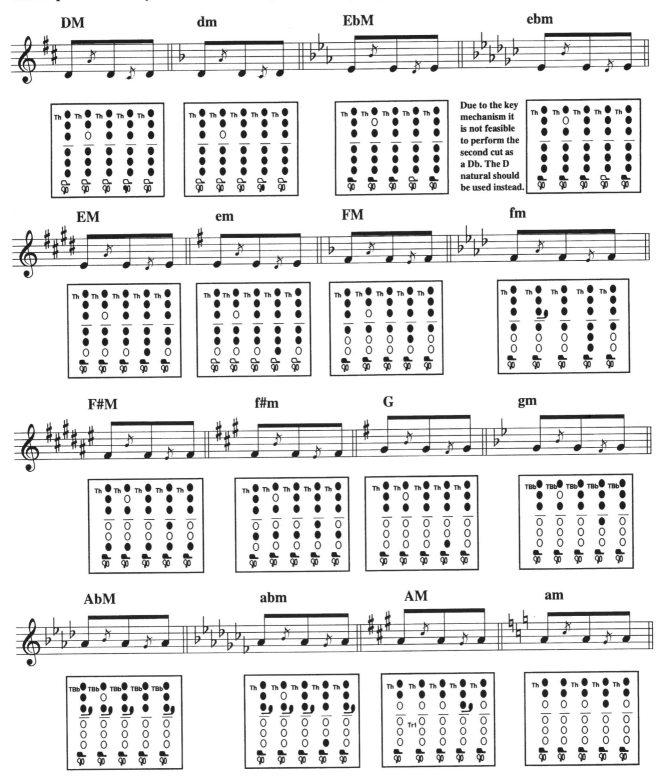

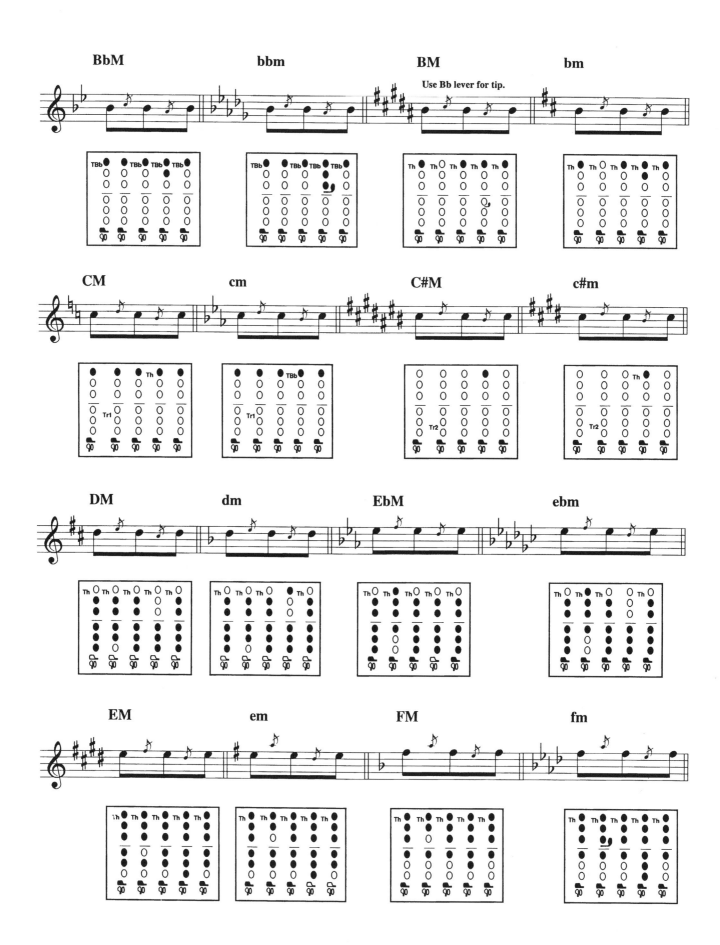

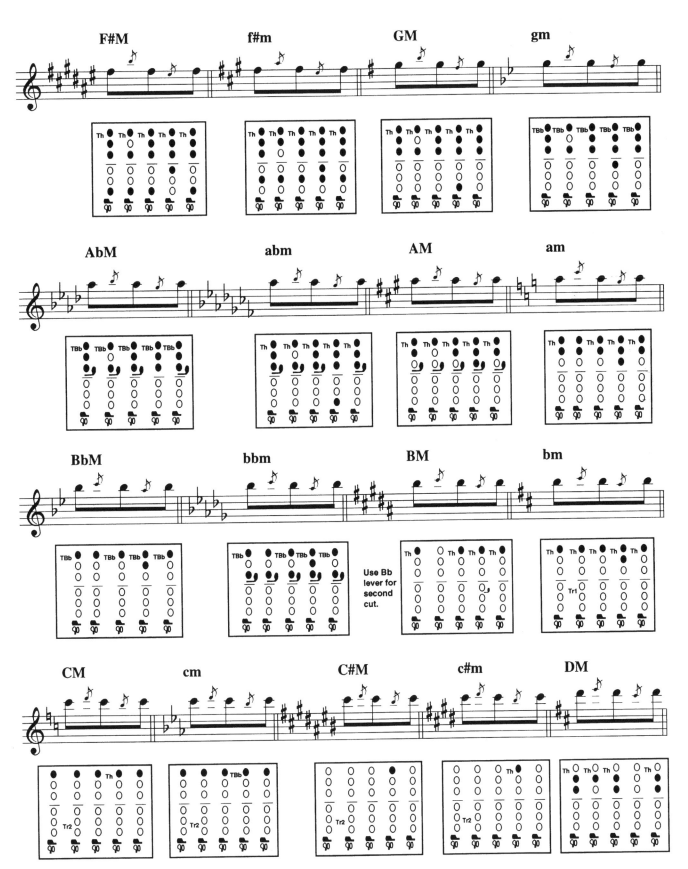

Note: It is possible to continue the range of rolled notes beyond high D.

Major Key/Cyclical Long Roll Exercise/
Simple Time

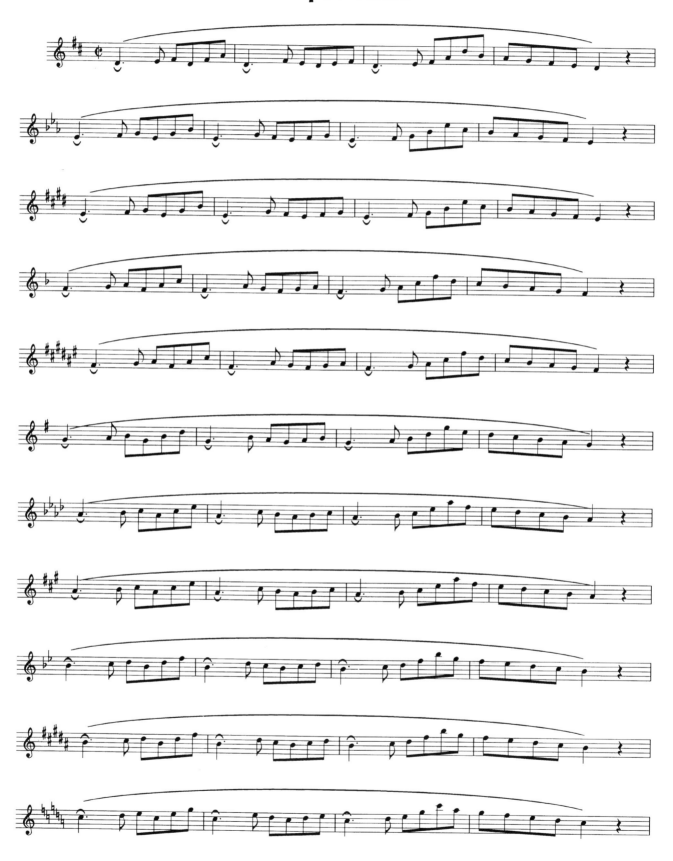

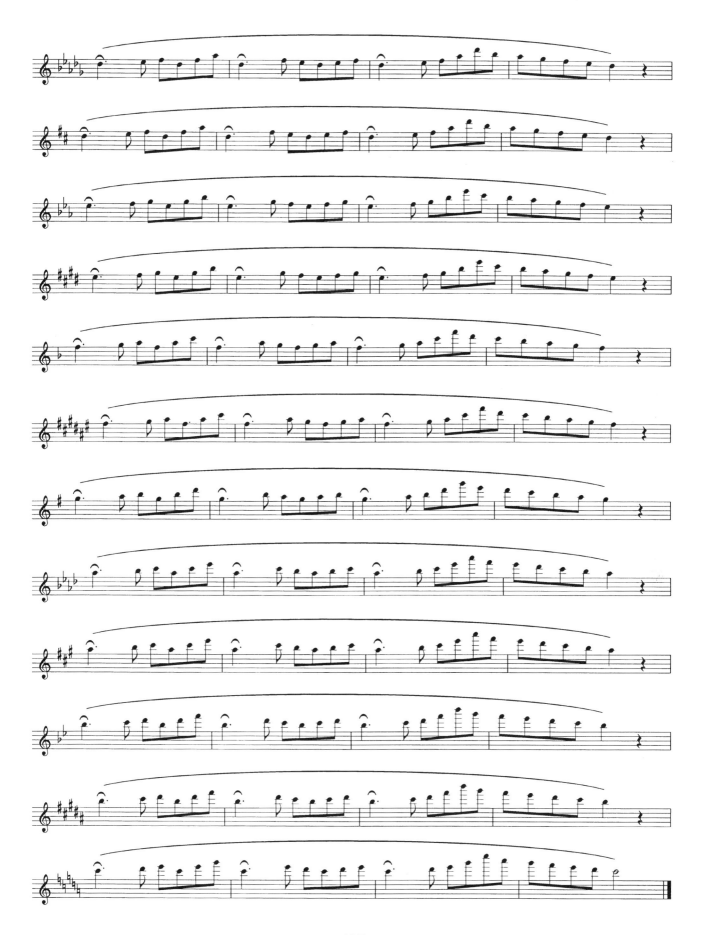

Major Key/Cyclical Long Roll Exercise/
Compound Time

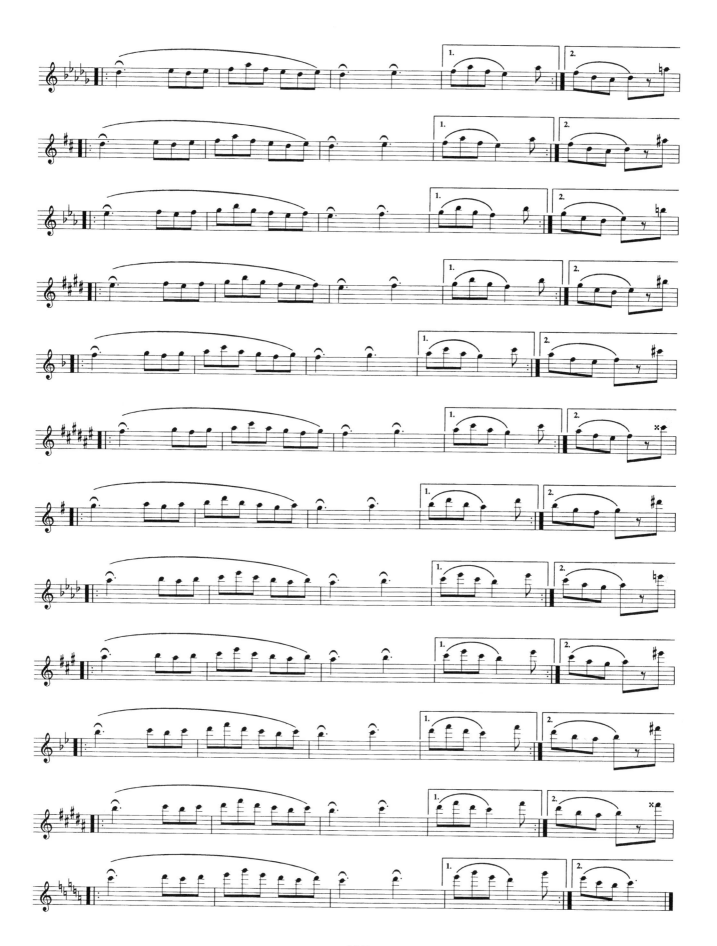

Long D Roll

Long E Flat Roll

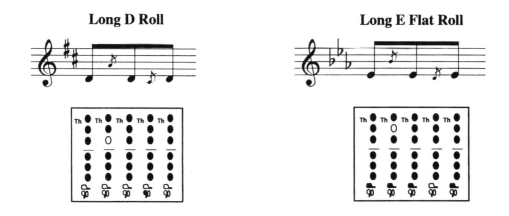

Roudledum

Merry Mary

Long John's Wedding

Long E Roll

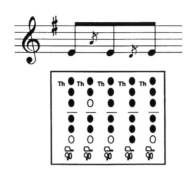

Dublin Streets

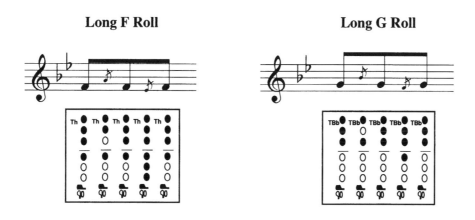

Long F Roll   **Long G Roll**

Galway Bay

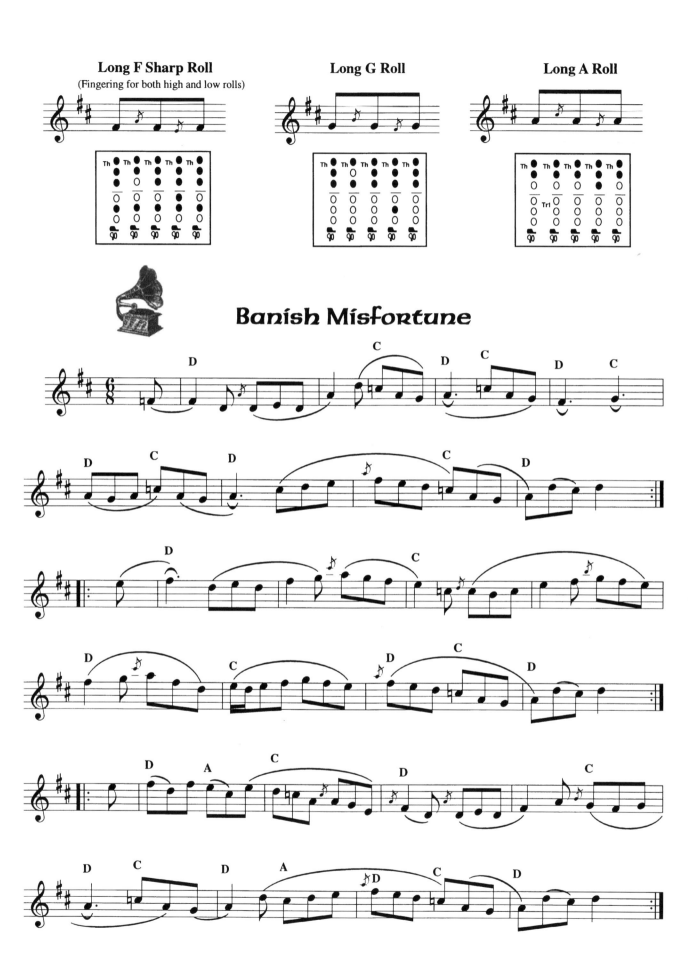

Long F Sharp Roll
(Fingering for both high and low rolls)

Long G Roll

Long A Roll

Banish Misfortune

Long A Flat Roll

(Fingering for both high and low rolls)

Long B Flat Roll

(Tip on A natural preferred)

Long E Flat Roll

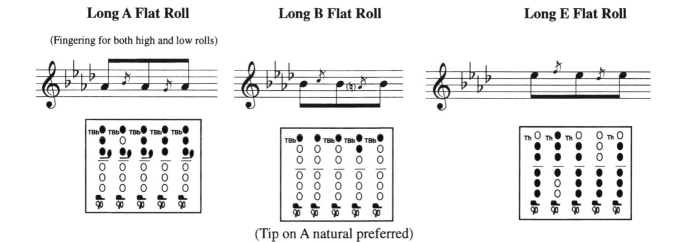

Miss Brown's Fancy

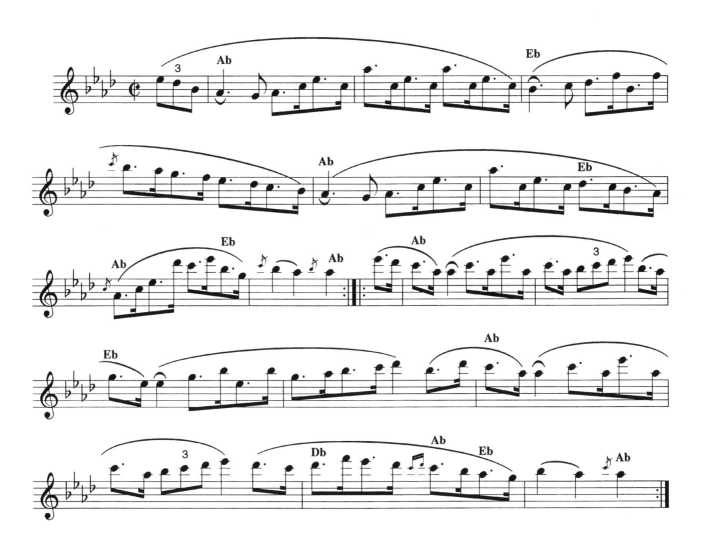

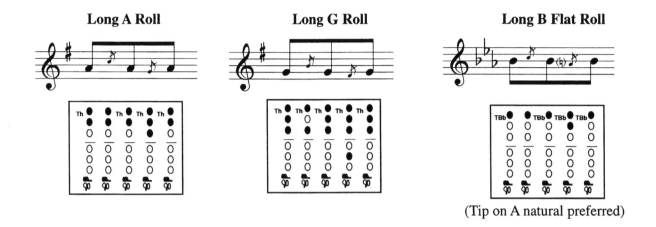

Long A Roll **Long G Roll** **Long B Flat Roll**

(Tip on A natural preferred)

The Angry Peeler

The Humours of Ballinafauna

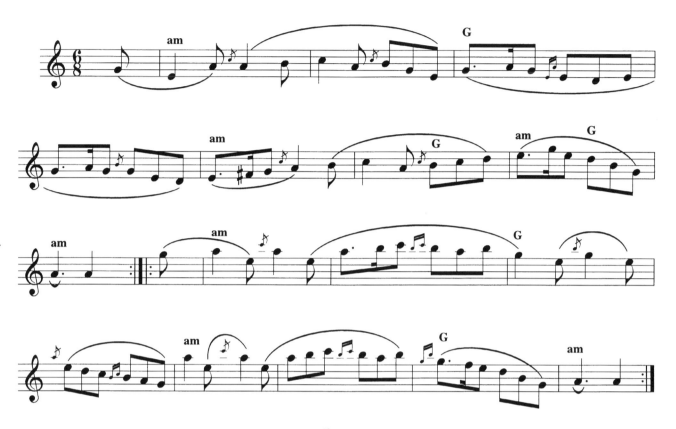

The Banks of Lough Gowna

Long B Roll

Long C Roll

Long C Sharp Roll

Long A Roll

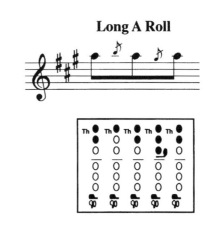

The Morning Star

Jackson's Bottle of Brandy

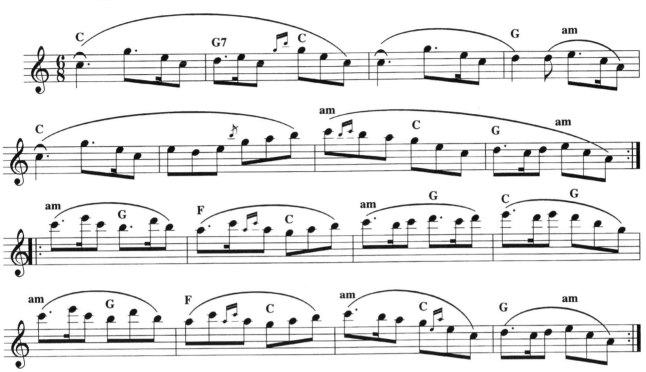

The Red Haired Hag

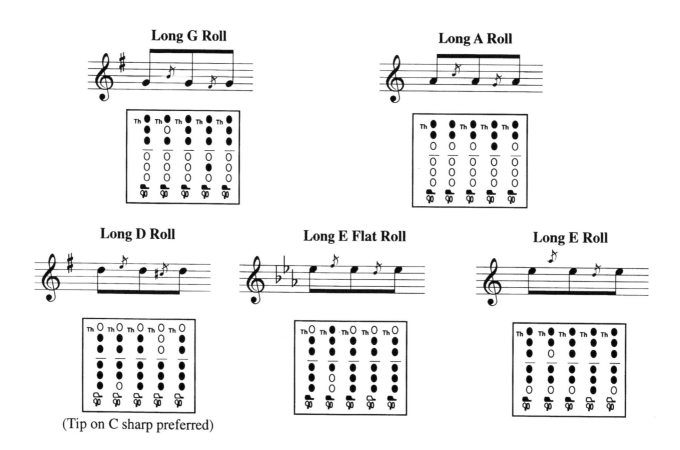

Long G Roll

Long A Roll

Long D Roll

Long E Flat Roll

Long E Roll

(Tip on C sharp preferred)

The Peeler's Jacket

The Rakes of Westmeath

Behind the Bush in the Garden

119

Long F Roll

Long F Sharp Roll

Long D Roll

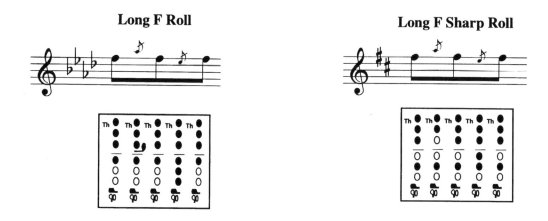

Young Francis Mooney

120

Fasten the Leg in Her

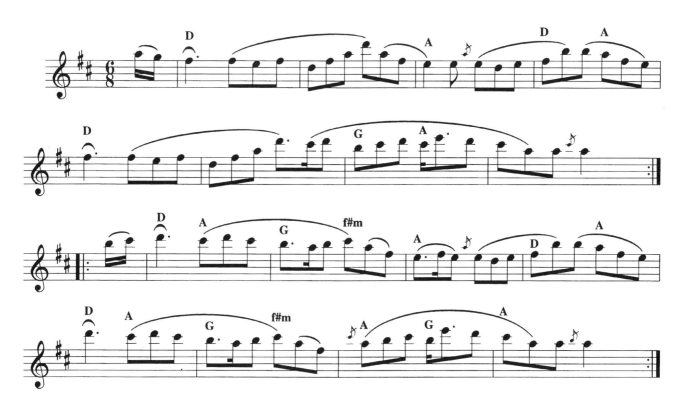

The Boys of Cappoquin

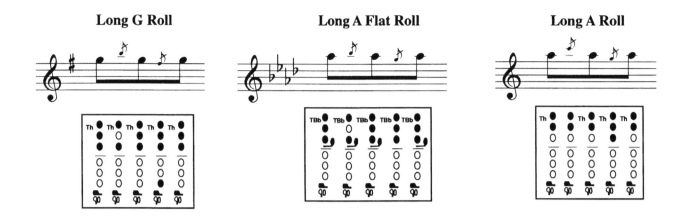

Long G Roll **Long A Flat Roll** **Long A Roll**

Nora O'Neill

The Woeful Widow

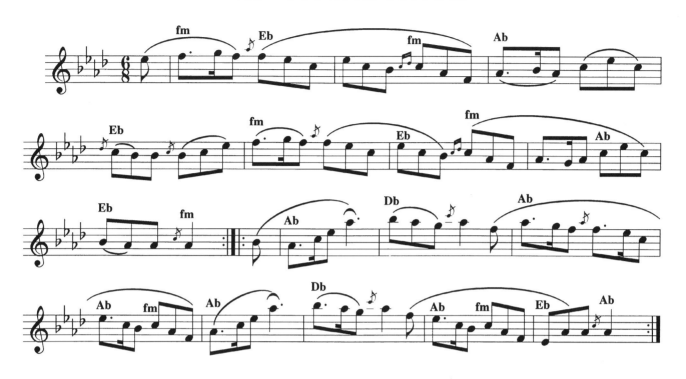

The Rambler from Clare

Long B Rolls **Long B Flat Roll** **Long C Roll**

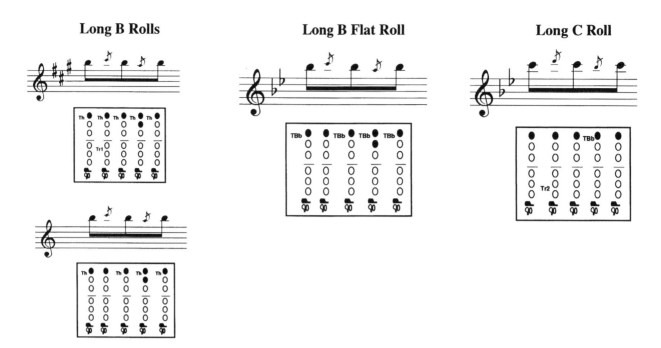

The Swallow's Tail

The Foot of the Mountain

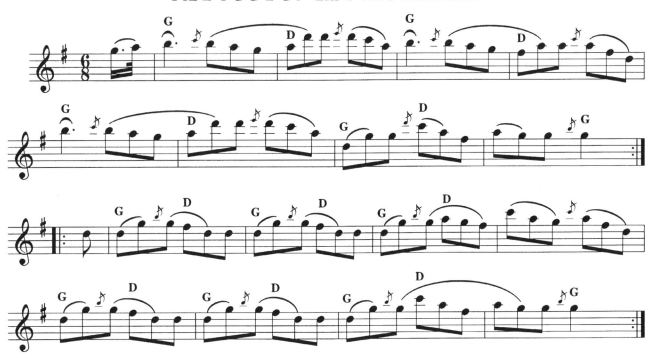

A Cloudy Morning

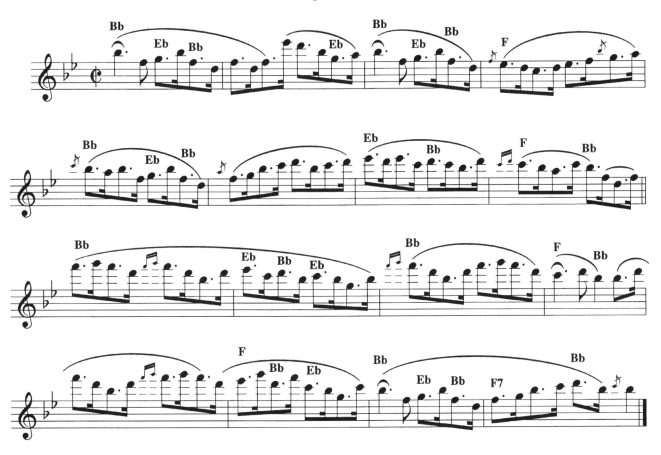

125

Cran

The **cran** is an ornament that is associated with piping. Since the manner in which notes are fingered on the pipes is similar to the flute, the technique of cranning may be applied to the flute. The cran is a series of cuts above the principal note. Each time a cut occurs a different finger is lifted, hence a different note will sound. The cran is usually performed on notes that have multiple fingerings for cuts. It may be substituted for a long or short roll, and will be notated as follows:

Cran in Simple Time

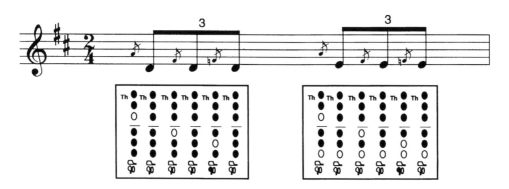

The effect of a cran may also be achieved when a cut is repeated as in the following example. At faster tempos the pitches of the cuts are almost indiscernible, and the rhythmic effect stays the same.

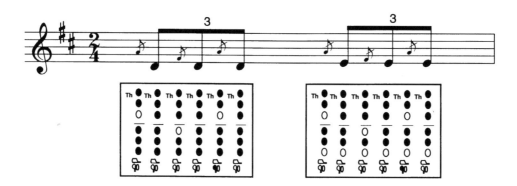

Cran in Compound Time

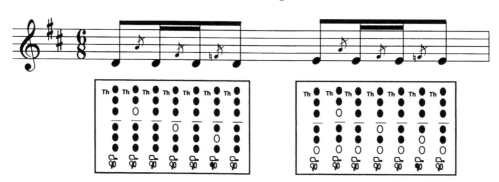

The Bucks of Oranmore

the process of variation

An important aspect of playing in the Irish style is the process of variation that occurs in nearly every solo performance. The music is essentially monophonic (i.e. single line melody), and a performance would seem monotonous unless some melodic variation occurred in addition to rhythmic alteration. The skilled player of traditional music is a master of theme and variation. Skeletal phrases are retained while melodic, ornamental, and rhythmic variations are applied. Add the process of variation to each piece you play. Eventually your custom variations will assist you in developing your own unique playing style.

melodic variation

Changes made in repeated versions of a piece employ many of the melodic ornaments familiar to classically trained players. More often than not, only small details of a melody are changed. Players who have learned via the aural tradition do not consciously label these melodic ornaments, yet they are fluent with their usage. Commonly used ornaments are described here for ease in identification and application.

Neighbor Tone(s)

A note or notes inserted directly above or below two notes of the same pitch.

Passing Tone(s)

A note or notes inserted between two notes that are separated by a larger interval. The passing tones are added to fill-in the interval and create a more stepwise motion from one note to the next. The process of adding passing tones can be reversed by eliminating notes to simplify the line.

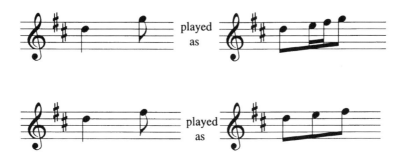

Added Chord Tone(s)

When ornamenting a note of long duration it is possible to insert notes belonging to chords implied by the melodic line. This is often done by ear when the player can hear suitable chordal accompaniments and add appropriate pitches. Guitar chords (when added above the musical line) can indicate suitable note additions. Observe how chord tones are inserted in the following example:

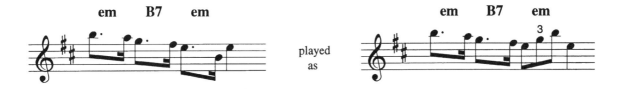

example for study

The following comparison of repeated sections in *Maids Aplenty* illustrates many of the typical changes that most players use when varying a melody:

a) Phrase/note changes for breathing (indicated by rest).
It is common practice to eliminate notes or change their duration in order to create a space where the player has ample time to breathe.
Compare measures 4, 6, 10, 14 and 16.

b) Slight melodic variation.
Passing tones and/or neighbor tones may be added to keep the rhythmic flow continuous. Compare measures 1 and 7.

c) Use of the triplet figure.
Compare measures 3, 6, 9 and 15.

d) Added grace notes.
Compare pick-up notes and measures 2, 8 and 12.

e) Interchange of rolls and simpler graced figures.
Compare measures 8, 9, 10, 11, 13 and 14.

f) Graced figures and triplets interchanged.
Staccato triplets substituted for rolls. Compare measures 1, 5, 14 and 15.

g) Added chord tones.
Compare measures 2, 4, 5, 6, 12, and 15.

Maids Aplenty

M.M./D.G.

130

 # Styles

At one time playing styles were localized to particular counties or regions in Ireland. Over the years recorded media and social mobility have allowed stylistic homogenization to take place such that these traits are no longer regionalized. Stylistic differences range from skeletal and simple melodies to highly ornamented renditions, and from long and legato phrases to short and crisply articulated phrases. The following examples represent three very different styles of flute playing. They illustrate the variety of ways ornamentation, phrasing, and rhythm may be combined to create a distinctive style. Remember that one of the great advantages of the folk tradition is that there is not a "correct way" to ornament a tune. A new variation is created each time a player performs. While this may seem like an obstacle to the novice it provides a continuous challenge even for the accomplished player.

Stylistic Traits: Preponderance of tonguing and sparse ornamentation. Skeletal version of melody with little rhythmic alteration.

Grandfather's Pet

Stylistic traits: Requires legato playing (long phrases with little tonguing and lots of breath control). Extra melodic note or triplet figure is used instead of other ornaments. Repeated notes under long phrases are articulated with a pulsation of the air stream rather than with the tongue. (See discussion of breath control for description of pulsations as they relate to vibrato.)

The Ewe Reel

132

Stylistic Traits: Use of shorter phrases. Heavily ornamented. Played at a fast tempo.

Over the Moor to Maggie

133

Slow Airs and Songs

The Irish culture has a rich solo song tradition, and the lyrical, haunting melodies of many Irish songs are often played as instrumental solos. The term "air" is often used to label a song, although more recently the connotation for an air is a slow melody of great beauty. There are different approaches to playing slow airs. One approach attempts to copy the vocal inflection of a singer. Players may refer to the text of a song and use the lyrics as a reference point from which to play in an expressive song-style. Ancient Gaelic songs were usually sung without accompaniment. The singer elaborated upon a skeletal melody by adding long melismas (several notes per syllable) as well as other traditional vocal ornaments. The rubato (varied) tempo and ornate embellishment make this one of the most difficult styles to learn, and playing in this manner requires concentrated study and listening to traditional singing styles.

Another approach to playing slow airs treats the music itself—the rise and fall of the musical line and its expressive qualities as a separate entity. This is used more often in the ensemble setting. When the air is sung or played with accompanying instruments it does not lend itself well to the improvisatory old-style of singing. An instrumental ensemble places more chordal and metric restrictions on the performer. Ornaments are used, but not to the same extent as in traditional solo performance practice.

The brief mention made here of the song tradition must be supplemented with additional study and careful listening. There is no substitution for studying recorded and live sources when learning airs.

Vibrato

An ornament that is frequently used in the performance of slow airs is the vibrato—the pulsation of a tone used to add expressive nuances to a musical line. Vibrato is used more often in slow airs than in dance music because the vibrato adds color and motion to notes of long duration.

There are two ways to achieve a vibrato on the flute:

1) Diaphragmatic Vibrato
Classical players are trained to create vibrato by altering the air stream with the use of the diaphragm (major muscle used for breathing) and/or throat musculature.

2) Fingered Vibrato
Another method used by folk players involves rapidly trilling open fingers to invoke subtle pitch variations (a piping technique which evolved from control of sound through a bellows rather than with the breath). The general rule on simple system flutes is to trill or waver the fingers above two or more holes below the last closed hole. The Boehm flute requires more experimentation as each flute responds according to its acoustical properties.

Diaphragmatic Vibrato

Gaining control of the diaphragm for purposes of expression can be learned through a regular practice regimen. As control over the musculature is achieved the vibrato may be added almost effortlessly by the performer. To practice the vibrato try the following exercise. Play a sustained pitch. Add evenly-spaced pulsations to the note by thrusting air from the diaphragm as if whispering the syllable "hah." Each thrust will cause a noticeable accentuation of the sustained note. Some players use the glottis or throat in this process.

Gradually increase the speed of the pulsations (as shown in the following example) until you are comfortable with the production and sound of the vibrato. The speed and use of the vibrato are largely a matter of personal taste. Listening to performances of slow airs by traditional players will give you a better idea of the various ways in which this expressive technique is used.

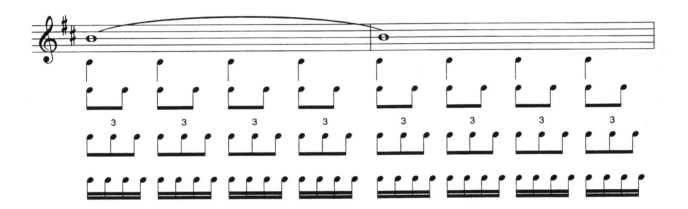

Note: It is also acceptable to trill on a note of long duration instead of using a vibrato. The trill is achieved by the rapid alternation of the principal note with the note directly above. It is notated with a trill symbol as in the example.

Fingered Vibrato

Wavering fingers over open tone holes is a traditional method of creating vibrato on the simple system flute. When transferred to the Boehm flute only certain notes will respond to this procedure due to the acoustical properties inherent in the Boehm key mechanism. The following chart offers a starting point for using fingered vibrato on the Boehm flute. **Experiment** with your instrument to find appropriate fingerings that will achieve the desired effect.

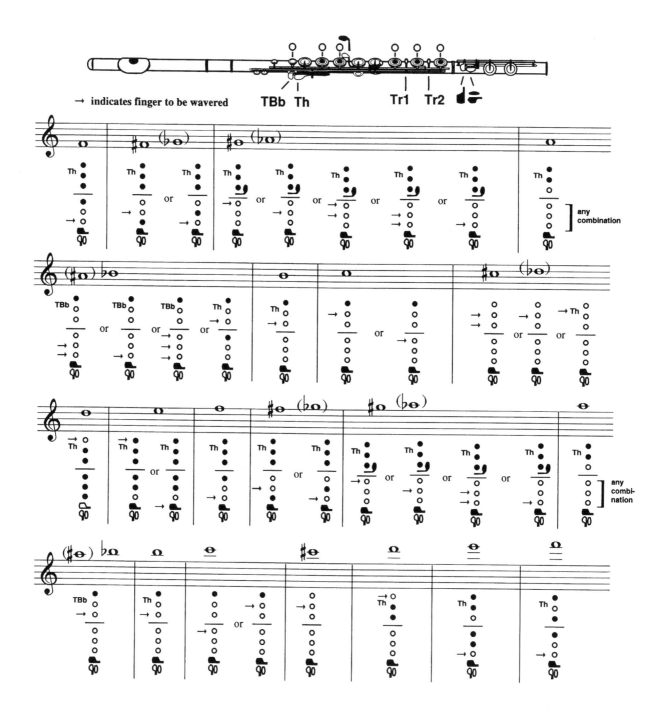

Sloan's Lamentation

Lord Mayo

The following song may be used as a model for instrumental performance.

Twas on a Winter's Evening

Text
(traditional)

1.
Twas on a winter's evening
When first came down the snow
Over hills and lofty mountains
The stormy winds did blow

A damsel she came tripping down
All in a drift of snow
With a baby in her arms
She knew not where to go

2.
She says my pretty baby
I'll warm you to my breast
For little does your father
Know how sore we are distressed

Hard-hearted as he is this night
If he knew how we did fare
He would take us in his arms
From the cruel and frosty air

3.
Hard-hearted was my father
That shut the door on me
But not so was my mother
For plainly she did see

That dark and stormy was the night
That pierced my heart with cold
And cruel was that false young man
Who sold his heart for gold

4.
Oh let me now be a warning
To all fair maids so gay
To ne'er believe false young men
No matter what they say

For they will kiss you and they'll court you
Till your fortune is their own
And they'll leave you there behind them
In sorrow to make moan

5.
Unto a silent grove she went
And there she did lie down
And she prayed for mercy on her soul
And the baby in her arms

She kissed her baby's cold cold lips
And laid it by her side
Turning her eyes to heaven
They both laid down and died

6.
Twas early next morning
That this fair maid was found
She and her little baby
Were frozen to the ground

Her tender mother tore her hair
And wept most bitterly
Saying love that serves two masters
Only ends in tragedy

The following ballad, attributed to the Scottish poet Robert Burns, is found in the second volume of a 1787 edition of Johnson's *Scots Musical Museum.* Another version is found in George Petrie's *Ancient Music of Ireland.* Petrie writes that

> *the same song, united to a melody unquestionably Irish has been equally,*
> *if not better, known in Ireland, and for an equal, if not longer, period: . . .*
> *of the claims of the two countries to this song, the Irish one is decidedly*
> *the stronger; for—without attaching much weight to the fact that the Scotch*
> *have been more in the habit of appropriating the music and poetry of Ireland*
> *than the Irish have been of taking such friendly liberties with theirs—the song,*
> *as sung in various parts of Ireland for more than a century, contains stanzas which,*
> *if not somewhat unreasonably assumed to be interpolations, very clearly establish*
> *it as of Irish origin.*

Petrie then gives two versions of the ballad (presented here) with the addendum "Having thus placed before my readers the Scottish and Irish versions of this ballad, I shall leave it to them to determine the relative claims of the two countries to its parentage . . . ."

The Winter it is Past

Scottish Version:

I

The winter it is past,
And the summer's come at last,
And the small birds sing on every tree;
The hearts of these are glad,
But mine is very sad,
For my lover has parted from me.

II

The rose upon the brier,
By the waters running clear,
May have charms for the linnet or the bee;
Their little loves are blest,
And their little hearts at rest,
But my lover is parted from me.

III

My love is like the sun,
In the firmament does run,
For ever is constant and true;
But his is like the moon,
That wanders up and down,
and every month it is new.

IV

All you that are in love,
And cannot it remove,
I pity the pains you endure;
For experience makes me know
That your hearts are full of woe—
A woe that no mortal can cure.

Irish Version

I

The winter it is past,
And the summer's come at last,
And the blackbirds sing on every tree;
The hearts of these are glad,
But mine is very sad,
Since my true love is absent from me.

II

The rose upon the brier,
By the water running clear,
Gives joy to the linnet and the bee;
Their little hearts are blest,
But mine is not at rest,
While my true love is absent from me.

III

A livery I'll wear,
And I'll comb down my hair,
And in velvet so green I'll appear;
And straight I will repair
To the Curragh of Kildare,
For it's there I'll find tidings of my dear.

IV

I'll wear a cap of black,
With a frill around my neck;
Gold rings on my fingers I'll wear;
It is this I'll undertake
For my true lover's sake;
He resides at the Curragh of Kildare.

V

I would not think it strange
Thus the world for to range,
If I only got tidings of my dear;
But here in Cupid's chain,
If I'm bound to remain,
I would spend my whole life in despair.

VI

My love is like the sun
That in the firmament does run,
And always proves constant and true;
But his is like the moon,
That wanders up and down,
And every month it is new.

VII

All you that are in love,
And cannot it remove,
I pity the pains you endure;
For experience makes me know
That your hearts are full of woe,
And a woe that no mortal can cure.

General Monroe's Lamentation

The Woods of Kilmurry

142

Pieces for Study

and Practice

The remaining portion of this text contains pieces for study and practice. An unornamented "standard" version of each piece is presented (I) along with an ornamented variant (II). You may find it easier to practice the given ornaments until you are confident enough to experiment with your own version. As you develop your own unique style of playing you will rely less upon the ornamented variant and return to the "standard" version as a reference point from which to work. A ceili-style piano accompaniment is also included for version II of each piece.

My Love She's But a Lassie Yet

I

II

144

Dogs Among the Bushes

Little Heathy Hill

Little Heathy Hill

II

King of the Fairies

I

King of the Fairies

Shandon Bells

The Ships are Sailing

151

The Drunken Sailor

I

153

The Drunken Sailor

II

155

The Groves Hornpipe

The Groves Hornpipe

II

The Jug of Punch

The Pigeon on the Gate

The Blackberry Blossom

I

II

The Mills are Grinding

My Love She's But a Lassie Yet

Dogs Among the Bushes

Little Heathy Hill

King of the Fairies

Shandon Bells

The Ships are Sailing

170

The Drunken Sailor

171

173

The Groves Hornpipe

175

The Jug of Punch

The Pigeon on the Gate

The Blackberry Blossom

178

The Mills are Grinding

179

Extended Cuts Fingering Chart

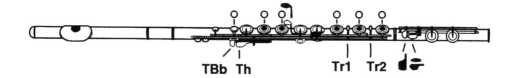

Note: Enharmonic spellings for every cut are not shown; however, a full chromatic range of notes is represented on the following chart.

180

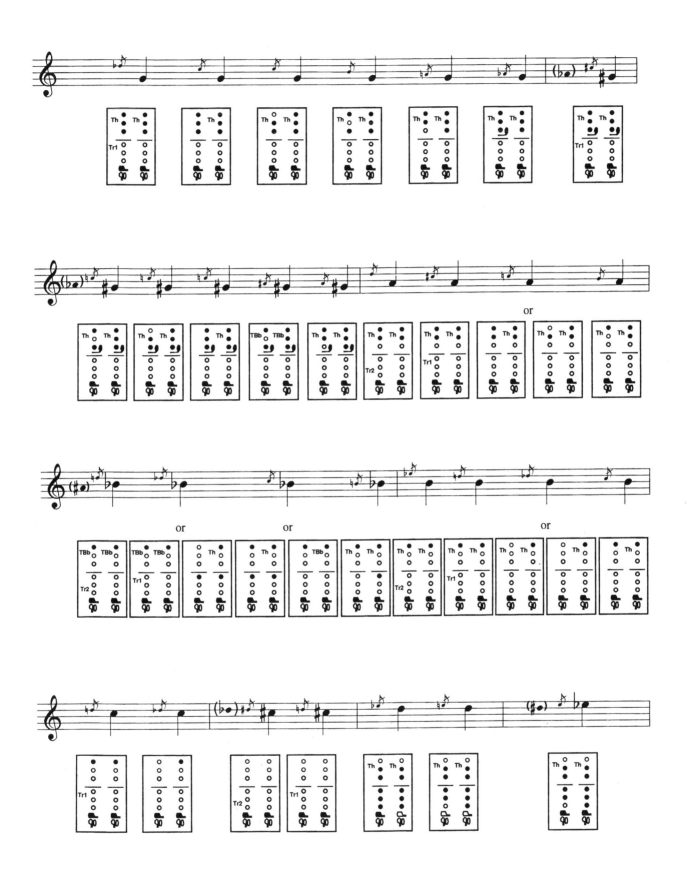

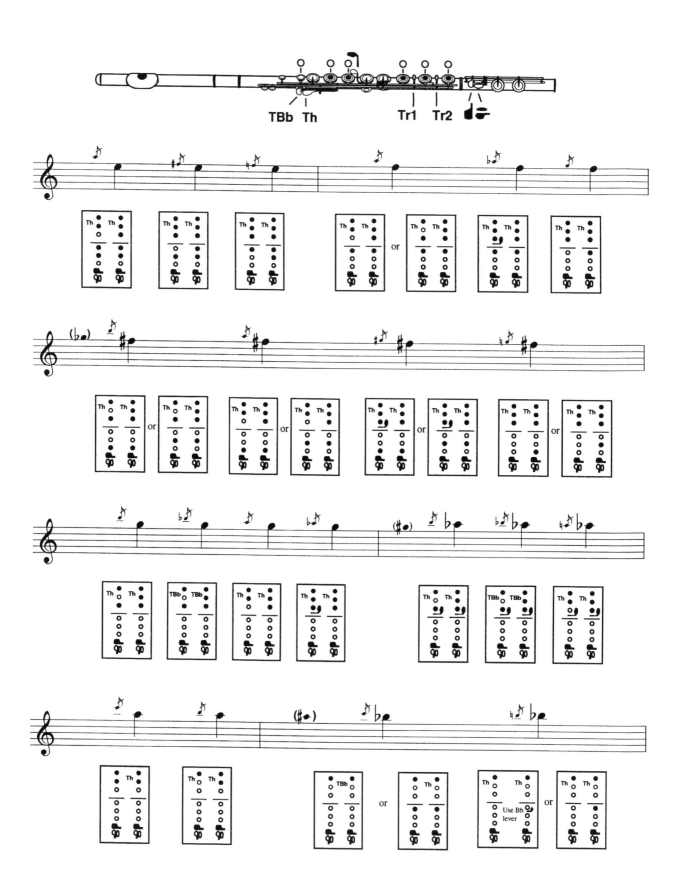

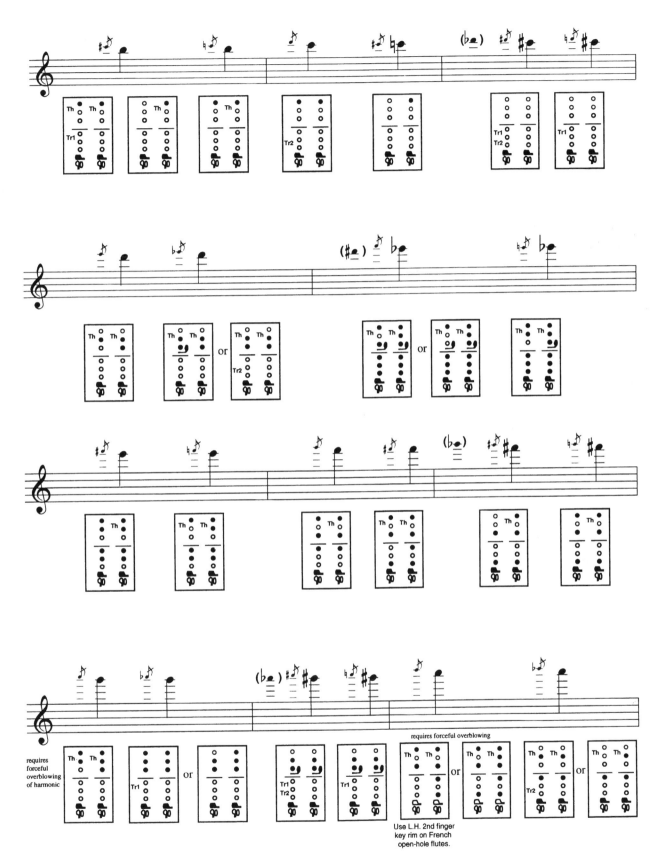

The range of notes that can be cut continues beyond high A.

Trill Chart

→ Indicates finger(s) to be trilled   TBb Th   Tr1   Tr2

trill chart continued

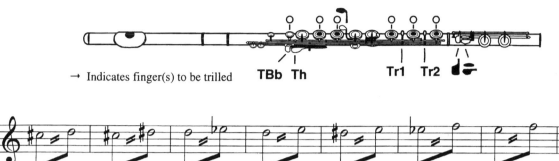

→ Indicates finger(s) to be trilled

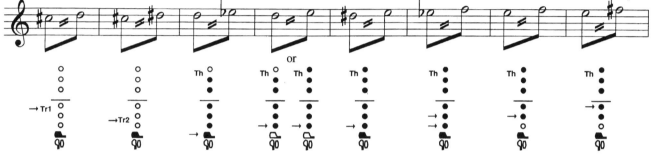

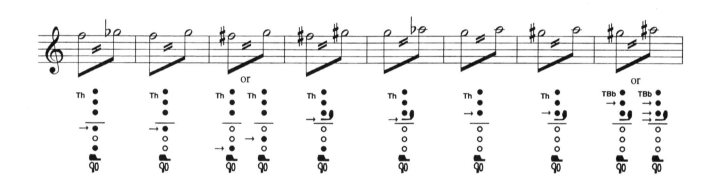

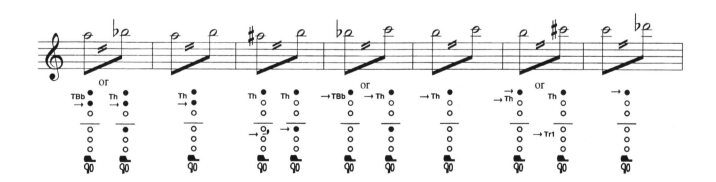

185

trill chart continued

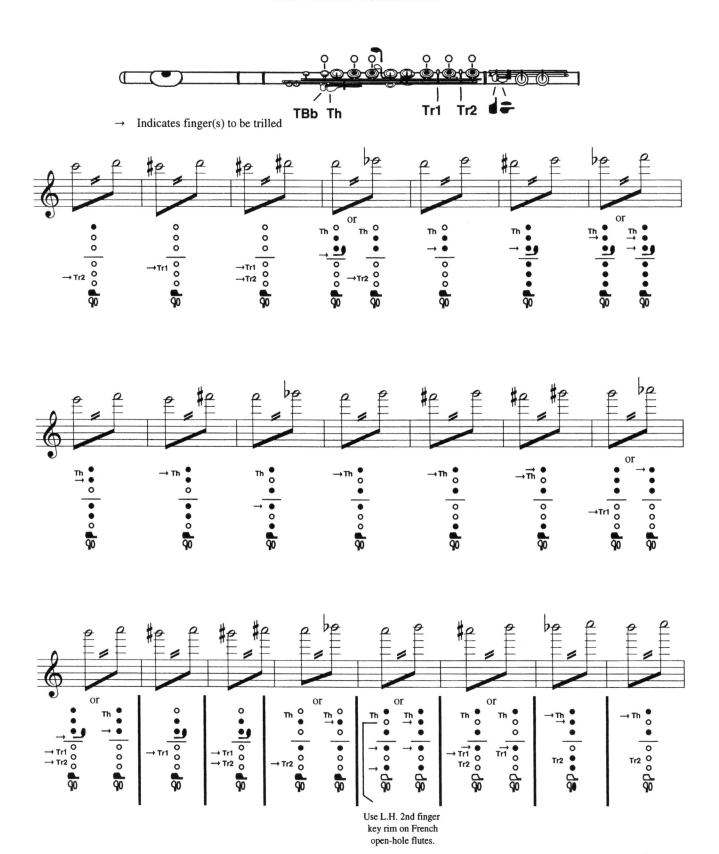

→ Indicates finger(s) to be trilled

Use L.H. 2nd finger
key rim on French
open-hole flutes.

Flute Fingering Chart

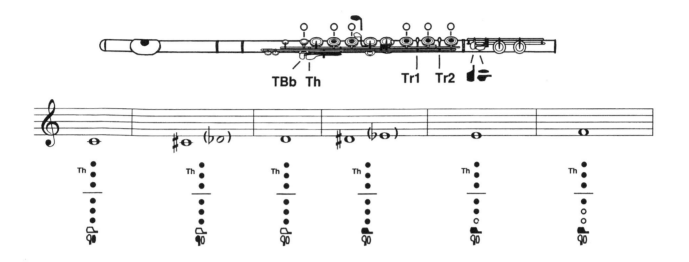

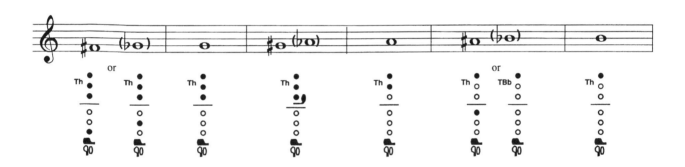

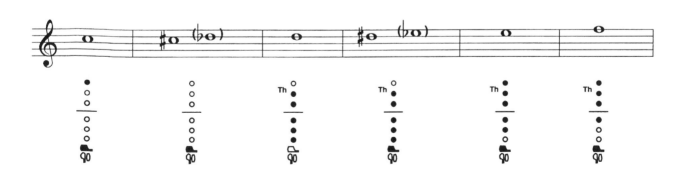

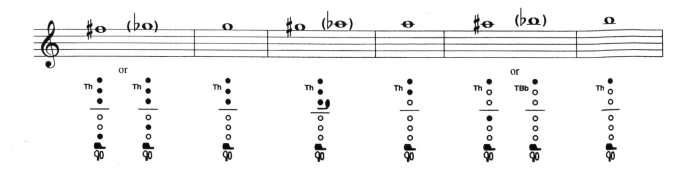

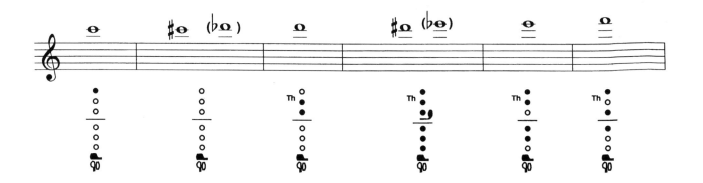

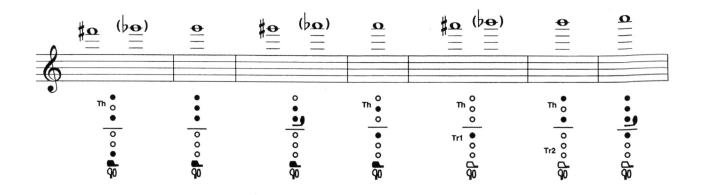

188

Index of Tunes by Genre

Hornpipes

Cronin's Rambles 15
Dick Sand's Hornpipe 63
Drunken Sailor, The 152-155
    piano 171-173
Early in the Morning 66
Fair and Forty 66
Galway Bay 111
Grove's Hornpipe, The 156-159
    piano 174-175
Hick's Hornpipe 64-65
Humphrey's Hornpipe 85
Miss Brown's Fancy 113
Tim the Turncoat 24
To the Men at Sea 28

Jigs

Double Jigs

Angry Peeler, The 114
Banish Misfortune 112
Banks of Lough Gowna, The 115
Come Along With Me 39
Connachtman's Rambles, The 12
Fasten the Leg in Her 121
Foot of the Mountain, The 125
Galway Tom 40-42
Grandfather's Pet 131
Jack of All Trades 61
Jackson's Bottle of Brandy 117
Jolly Corkonian, The 46-47
Julia McMahon 53
Long John's Wedding 109
Merry Mary 109
Miss Grant's Jig 11
Rambler from Clare, The 123
Red Haired Hag, The 117
Shandon Bells 150
    piano 169
Wellington's Advance 45
Woeful Widow, The 123
Young Francis Mooney 120

Single Jigs

Behind the Bush in the Garden 119
Humours of Ballinafauna, The 115
Lovely Lad, The 54
Shady Lane, The 13

Slip or Hop Jigs

Comb Your Hair and Curl It 14
Dublin Streets 110
Rakes of Westmeath, The 119
Roudledum 108
Tipperary Hills 37

Polka

My Love She's But a Lassie Yet 144
    piano 164

Reels

Avonmore, The 84
Blackberry Blossom, The 162
    piano 178
Bloom of Youth, The 38, 91
Boys of Cappoquin, The 121
Bucks of Oranmore, The 127
Callan Lasses, The 78
Captain Kelly's Reel 92
Clancy's Fancy Reel 94
Cloudy Morning, A 125
Coming Over the Hills 96
Dogs Among the Bushes 145
    piano 165
Dublin Lasses, The 81
Ewe Reel, The 132
Flower of the Flock, The 16
Green Jacket, The 77
Greenlefe Inn, The 82
Happy Days of Youth, The 43
Johnny's Wedding 44
Jolly Seven, The 89

Reels continued

Jug of Punch, The 160
     piano 176
Leaves of Three 58
Magpie's Nest, The 55
Maid at the Churn, The 98
Maid in the Cherry Tree, The 87
Maids Aplenty 130
Mason's Apron, The 86
Mills are Grinding, The 163
     piano 179
Miltown Maid, The 79
Morning Star, The 116
New Demesne, The............................. 90
Nora O'Neill 122
Old Grey Gander, The 95
O'Reilly's Greyhound 99
Over the Moor to Maggie 133
Peeler's Jacket, The 118
Peggy on the Settle 88
Pigeon on the Gate, The 161
     piano 177
Rose in the Garden, The 59
Ships are Sailing, The 151
     piano 170
Steam Packet, The 93
Strawberry Blossom, The 97
Swallow's Tail, The 124
Take Your Choice 21, 80
Touch Me If You Dare 83
Western Lasses, The 56-57
Your Mother's Fair Pet 22

Set Dances

Blackbird, The 18
Job of Journey Work, The.................... 17
King of the Fairies 148-149
     piano 167-168

Slow Airs and Songs

General Monroe's Lamentation 142
Light from Ennistimon 28
Little Heathy Hill 146-147
     piano 166
Lord Mayo 137
Sloan's Lamentation 137
Twas on a Winter's Evening 138
Winter it is Past, The.......................... 140
Woods of Kilmurry, The 142

Index of Tunes

Angry Peeler, The 114
Avonmore, The 84

Banish Misfortune 112
Banks of Lough Gowna, The 115
Behind the Bush in the Garden 119
Blackberry Blossom, The 162
    piano 178
Blackbird, The 18
Bloom of Youth, The 38, 91
Boys of Cappoquin, The 121
Bucks of Oranmore, The 127

Callan Lasses, The 78
Captain Kelly's Reel 92
Clancy's Fancy Reel 94
Cloudy Morning, A 125
Comb Your Hair and Curl It 14
Come Along With Me 39
Coming Over the Hills 96
Connachtman's Rambles, The 12
Cronin's Rambles 15

Dick Sand's Hornpipe 63
Dogs Among the Bushes 145
    piano 165
Drunken Sailor, The 152-155
    piano 171-173
Dublin Lasses, The 81
Dublin Streets 110

Early in the Morning 66
Ewe Reel, The 132

Fair and Forty 66
Fasten the Leg in Her 121
Flower of the Flock, The 16
Foot of the Mountain, The 125

Galway Bay 111
Galway Tom 40-42
General Monroe's Lamentation 142
Grandfather's Pet 131
Green Jacket, The 77
Greenlefe Inn, The 82

Grove's Hornpipe, The 156-159
    piano 174-175

Happy Days of Youth, The 43
Hick's Hornpipe 64-65
Humours of Ballinafauna, The 115
Humphrey's Hornpipe 85

Jack of All Trades 61
Jackson's Bottle of Brandy 117
Job of Journey Work, The 17
Johnny's Wedding 44
Jolly Corkonian, The 46-47
Jolly Seven, The 89
Julia McMahon 53
Jug of Punch, The 160
    piano 176

King of the Fairies 148-149
    piano 167-168

Leaves of Three 58
Light from Ennistimon 28
Little Heathy Hill 146-147
    piano 166
Long John's Wedding 109
Lord Mayo 137
Lovely Lad, The 54

Magpie's Nest, The 55
Maid at the Churn, The 98
Maid in the Cherry Tree, The 87
Maids Aplenty 130
Mason's Apron, The 86
Merry Mary 109
Mills are Grinding, The 163
    piano 179
Miltown Maid, The 79
Miss Brown's Fancy 113
Miss Grant's Jig 11
Morning Star, The 116
My Love She's But a Lassie Yet 144
    piano 164

New Demesne, The 90
Nora O'Neill 122

Old Grey Gander, The 95
O'Reilly's Greyhound 99
Over the Moor to Maggie 133

Peeler's Jacket, The 118
Peggy on the Settle 88
Pigeon on the Gate, The 161
        piano 177

Rakes of Westmeath, The 119
Rambler from Clare, The 123
Red Haired Hag, The 117
Rose in the Garden, The 59
Roudledum 108

Shandon Bells 150
        piano 169
Shady Lane, The 13
Ships are Sailing, The 151
        piano 170

Sloan's Lamentation 137
Steam Packet, The 93
Strawberry Blossom, The 97
Swallow's Tail, The 124

Take Your Choice 21, 80
Tim the Turncoat................................... 24
Tipperary Hills 37
To the Men at Sea 28
Touch Me If You Dare 83
Twas on a Winter's Evening 138

Wellington's Advance 45
Western Lasses, The 56-57
Winter it is Past, The........................... 140
Woeful Widow, The 123
Woods of Kilmurry, The 142

Young Francis Mooney........................... 120
Your Mother's Fair Pet 22

For those who have a further interest in learning a repertoire of traditional Irish music the authors recommend *Mel Bay's Complete Irish Tin Whistle Book* and CD. This book/CD package is similar in format to the *Complete Irish Flute Book*/CD; however, it contains an entirely different set of tunes, all of which are within the range of the flute. Music for the Irish tin whistle may be played on the flute due to the similarity of fingerings and range of the instruments. Flutists of all ages can easily learn and play the tin whistle. It is a delightful alternative for beginners and in the hands of a skilled player it can become an instrument for the virtuoso player.

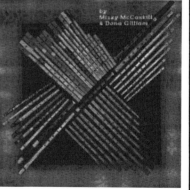

MEL BAY'S COMPLETE
írish tín whistle book